The World of Waiters

The World of Waiters

GERALD MARS
and
MICHAEL NICOD

London
GEORGE ALLEN & UNWIN
Boston   Sydney

George Allen & Unwin (Publishers) Ltd,
40 Museum Street, London WC1A 1LU, UK

George Allen & Unwin (Publishers) Ltd,
Park Lane, Hemel Hempstead, Herts HP2 4TE, UK

Allen & Unwin Inc.,
9 Winchester Terrace, Winchester, Mass 01890, USA

George Allen & Unwin Australia Pty Ltd,
8 Napier Street, North Sydney, NSW 2060, Australia

First published in 1984

British Library Cataloguing in Publication Data

Mars, Gerald
    The world of waiters.
1. Table service
I. Title   II. Nicod, Michael
642'.6   TX925
ISBN 0-04-301178-0
ISBN 0-04-301182-9 Pbk

Set in 11 on 13 point Garamond by Computape (Pickering) Ltd, North Yorkshire
and printed in Great Britain by Biddles Ltd, Guildford, Surrey

Contents

Acknowledgements

A study such as this can hardly be considered the sole work of the authors, even though we willingly accept responsibility for its defects. Professional anthropologists will undoubtedly recognise our massive debt to Mary Douglas and it is a pleasure to record our gratitude to her – not only for her ideas but for her generous encouragement. Unfortunately Erving Goffman, our other principal source of inspiration, is no longer with us. His influence will be evident to readers who know his work.

Much of this material has been discussed at different times and in different places with a variety of professional colleagues. In particular, however, we would like to thank those colleagues who attend seminars at Middlesex Polytechnic's Centre for Occupational and Community Research and who commented on several chapters in early draft form. Most particularly we would thank Peter Mitchell whose advice and detailed knowledge of the industry were constantly and generously available at all stages from planning through to analysis. Stuart Henry has been a constant adviser and a generous critic while Geoff Dench and Ralph Grillo both made valuable suggestions. All their efforts followed the award of grant HR4307 from the Social Science Research Council for which we are extremely grateful.

We owe, of course, a considerable debt to people in the industry – both those who participated knowingly in our work and those who did not. We cannot for obvious reasons mention their names. One, however, stands out above all and confirms the findings of other workers – that one alert, empathic and intelligent informant can mean the difference between a disasterous field experience and one that is fruitful. 'Molly' was the ideal informant: we respect her wish for anonymity – regretfully!

Neither of us find it easy to organise our material and here too our luck held. We were fortunate to have the assistance of Cathy Hopkins who not only massively 'tidied up' our initial efforts but offered advice on content and even supplied comparative case material. Further effective tidying – to put it mildly – was supplied by Adam Sisman and Mary Trewby while Daphne Clench typed numerous drafts with cheerful, if frenzied, resignation. It is a pleasure to record an especial debt to our agent, Frances Kelly, for involvement and expertise well beyond the norm.

Finally our wives Lynfa Nicod and Valerie Mars have lived with this work for so long that 'acknowledgement' can no longer describe the extent of our obligations.

Preface

This book is by two anthropologists and is based on a research programme designed by Mars and fieldwork carried out by Nicod, who 'went native' as a waiter in the restaurants of five British hotels over an aggregate period of nearly two years. They ranged from a fashionable and highly prestigious international hotel in London's West End, to a vulgar holiday hotel that was more 'sing-along' that *soignée*.

We can generalise from what might appear a limited sample because our hotels cover a wide range of variables. As well as choosing them on the basis of class we took account of size, setting – whether they were urban, metropolitan or seaside – and of price. And as our findings emerged they were checked for general applicability. The fieldwork took place with interruptions for analysis, in the three years to 1979 and the analysis has continued into the 1980s. Names of hotels and of informants have not been revealed.

Mars and Nicod became involved in this research in different ways. Mars had had extensive experience since the 1960s as an anthropologist in various industries and had spent time before that as a waiter in hotels and restaurants at the lower and medium end of the market. He had researched and written throughout the following decade on aspects of hotel and restaurant organisation and on pilferage and gyping as normal aspects of work. In 1976, with Peter Mitchell, he published for the Open University the first account of the UK hotel industry that took account of rewards and their allocation – both legitimate and otherwise – as a basis for understanding the industry.

The Open University study raised questions that could only be answered by direct involvement in hotels from the inside. These had to do with secrets: with whether permitted pilferage is equally regarded as a regular part of wages throughout the whole of this industry; with whether indeed we have more than one industry; with trying to tease out how waiters are trained, not only in how to carry out their formal tasks but in how they are taught the informal side of their work – the fiddles and tricks of the trade.

Meanwhile, at University College, London, Nicod was engaged with Mary Douglas on the study of dietary systems. Together they had elicited the rules which govern the presentation of food within British homes. This was the first systematic attempt to understand the delicate transactions which determine how idiosyncratic likes and dislikes take priority in normal domestic eating; how the rules governing diet are linked to other aspects of family social systems and with what makes these rules different from those found in restaurants (Douglas, 1972: Douglas and Nicod, 1974).

This work raised interesting questions that begged investigation to do with the idea of service. We wanted to know how far the service ideal varied from the norm in different parts of the industry and with the transactions these involved. We wanted to examine how waiters learn to stereotype their customers and why, and with whether and how customers in their turn can manipulate waiters.

The occupational world of waiters is a world of rites and rituals, of status passages, of minutely divided hierarchies, of closely guarded and secret knowledge that can never be understood from the customers' side of the green baize door. These are the kind of concerns central to the interests of anthropologists – though normally they do not explore them in workplaces of the industrial West. But the anthropologist's method of work – of direct involvement in the day-to-day affairs of the people they study, as well as by close observation of their activities – seemed to us to offer the best means of learning about this industry's inner life.

A grant to Mars from the UK Social Science Research Council provided funds for Nicod's employment as a fieldworker. Armed with two salaries, we prepared for his double life.

1

Going Native In Restaurants

... never be sorry for a waiter. Sometimes when you sit in a
restaurant still stuffing yourself half an hour after closing time you
feel that the tired waiter at your side must surely be despising you.
But he is not. He is not thinking as he looks at you 'what an overfed
lout'. He is thinking 'one day when I have saved enough money I
shall be able to imitate that man'. He is ministering to a kind of
pleasure he thoroughly understands and admires. And that is why
waiters are seldom socialists, have no effective trade union and will
work twelve hours a day seven days a week... They are snobs and
they find the rather servile nature of their work rather congenial.
(George Orwell, *Down and Out in Paris and London*, 1933)

All of us eat out – some of us consistently and some more
infrequently. But the experience, like lovemaking or travel,
always varies – no two occasions are ever quite the same. From the
beginning, our research for this book was concerned to tease out
the rules that lie behind these differences – we wanted, in short, to
learn how restaurants *really* work. We aimed to uncover the signs
that waiters look for when they stereotype their customers and why
indeed they need to stereotype them at all. We needed to know
why some people seem always to be ushered to the best tables and
by royally treated, whilst others have almost physically to throw
themselves at a waiter's feet before he will even acknowledge their
presence. Does the service people receive depend merely upon how
they are dressed or has it more to do with the class of the place? Is it
linked somehow with a customer's 'bearing' or is it just that he
seems likely to be a good tipper? Why should women be especially

prone to be ignored or tucked away in a corner? And what can the customer do successfully to play the system?

As our work progressed we learned the answers to these questions and to many more. We learned just why it is that we should be so firmly ushered to one table rather than another. We came to recognise what lies behind the apparently benevolent recommendation that 'the roast beef is particularly good tonight, sir', or why sometimes the service should be an 'over the top' theatrical performance while at others it is part of a cool and collected experience.

But to answer questions such as these, one cannot just walk into restaurants and question their staffs. One needs both a plan and a method. We believe the methods anthropologists use to study, say, the New Guinea Highlanders are also ideally suited to a study of the 'tribe' of waiters at work in Western hotels.

The main technique anthropologists use is to live among the people they are studying and to participate as far as possible in their day-to-day life. In this way, they aim to build up a picture of the subjects' cultural world.

In particular, they attempt to elicit the key values and norms (often unstated) on which social life is based. And in doing this they must try to avoid ethnocentricity – letting their own values distort their perceptions – the main pitfall for untrained observers.

Traditionally, the anthropological approach is 'holistic': the researcher does not focus on a single activity, but surveys a whole range of activities and their interconnections. A study of a work-group is not limited to looking at the work its members perform; rather, their work *and* leisure *and* community life are researched, and the ways in which these are interlinked. This type of information can only be obtained by participating in and by direct observation of every kind of behaviour as it occurs – a method which is more reliable than people's retrospective or anticipatory reports of their own behaviour (as in the standard sociological research technique of interview/questionnaire and the study of existing data).

This 'participant-observer' approach has further advantages.

2

Many forms of behaviour are so taken for granted that it would not occur to the subjects or even the best local informant to report them. The (ideally) detached anthropologist, however, taking nothing for granted, would record them: some of these apparently insignificant facts may be seen later to be of key importance for understanding the social structure and cultural values of the subjects. There are occasions, too, when people are unwilling to put certain facts on record because they fear the consequences of exposing themselves to the scrutiny – and judgement – of others. This is especially so where illicit activity is concerned – and every occupation has its share of this. Again, many people simply will not, or cannot, spare the time to be interviewed, which presents a considerable obstacle to obtaining a 'balanced' sample of informants.

Anthropologists, as both participants and observers, then, are well equipped to look at occupations using the approaches they would adopt for the study of a tribal society. The framework within which they try to understand and interpret the way people behave at work, is constructed from the following questions:

1 *Recruitment and initiation*: Who are recruited? How are they recruited? How are people trained to accept the culture of the industry and the institution?
2 *Power relationships*: How is power exercised? Who exercises it? What social controls operate to enforce it?
3 *Relationships inside/outside*: What kinds of relationship exist within the group, and between its members and those outside it? How are these relationships marked, defined and emphasised, by dress, for example, or work functions, age, sex?
4 *Ideology*: What is the body of expectations and values shared by the members of the group? How are these transmitted and perpetuated?

When an anthropologist conducts this kind of study, whether the subjects be the Watusi or Western waiters, the cornerstone of

3

his research is enthnography, the careful description of another culture in its own terms. Ethnography is based on three important principles which anthropologists have derived from their studies of non-Western societies and which have guided our own study of hotel waiters. These are:

1 *Behaviour is assumed not to be random.* Human behaviour is patterned activity. Every human group creates its own reality and has a shared culture. Behaviour within each culture is generated by a set of ground rules — a way of looking at the world, judging how to organise one's behaviour and interpreting the significance of what others do.

2 *The tendency for behaviour to fall into patterns stems largely from political and economic concerns.* Cultural rules are often accepted without thought. In fact, it is potentially dangerous for those under investigation to fully understand why they behave as they do. Despite the complexity of the rules, people are taught and learn to classify other individuals in such a way that it is possible to anticipate how they will behave and how to interact with them in a manner appropriate to their political and economic status (for instance, whether they should show them respect, familiarity, or contempt).

   A fundamental feature of every society is that people categorise their social world, usually with names — so they will describe people as 'co-wife', 'mother's brother', 'big man'; or, nearer home in hotels, 'commis waiter', 'sous chef', or 'receptionist'. Given these cultural rules and how they operate within these constraints, it makes sense to speak of a 'social system'.

3 *The patterns that develop are linked: if one part of the system varies, other linked variations can be expected.* When these assumptions, which are almost too deep to be explicit in 'tribal' societies, are applied to our own workplaces they shed an unfamiliar light upon people and their activities, and allow us to see them in new ways. This raises questions about the relationship of one aspect of work to the rest of people's occupational cultures.

Technology here is particularly important. A simple change in technology for instance, can often produce extensive and often unanticipated results. The introduction of 'catering systems', for instance, has reduced the autonomy of chefs (and their power to fiddle the costs of food purchases) which has led to an overall loss of prestige and a growth in their union membership (see Chivers 1973).

The aim of our research has been to record the hotel and its restaurant world through the eyes of waiters and to describe its culture in their own terms. Of course, this view is a limiting one: it focuses on a small cultural world from a single perspective. This does not mean that other perspectives – that of hotel managers or of customers, for instance – are unimportant: they would undoubtedly yield interesting data on hotel culture as well. However, our purpose was not to build up an all-inclusive picture of hotels, but to look at them from the single viewpoint of the individuals who provide the service in a service occupation.

Why Hotels?

In his classic study of the hotel industry in Chicago during the 1940s, W. F. Whyte (1948, p.v) wrote:

> In the past, students of human relations in industry have concentrated their attention on the factory, and important advances have been made in that field. However, the proportion of our population employed in the service industries has been steadily increasing, so that those who wish to understand the functioning of American society must also turn their attention in this direction.

Twenty years after Whyte, Miller and Rice (1967, p.45) made the point that the need still existed for research in this neglected area:

> There remains a tendency, among theorists and practitioners alike, to look upon the organization of production operations as central

5

and typical, and to assume that the principles of delegation and control that have emerged constitute general laws of organization . . . We believe that examination of non-productive organization can help us to see production organization in a new light and to question some prevalent assumptions . . . (and that) in the context of a general theory of organization the conventional factory situation, far from being prototypical, is a special case.

The framework within which this study was planned and developed derived from concepts and hypotheses which Mars (1973; 1974; 1982) and Mars and Mitchell (1976; 1977) had speculated were important in trying to understand the hotel as an organisation. However, we also hoped to follow Miller and Rice's argument, inasmuch as the evidence that was likely to emerge might shed light on the various assumptions and claims of organisation theories.

Questions about the kind of indulgences permitted, the limits prescribed, the techniques of rule-making and rule-breaking, the ratio of formalised to unformalised types of reward, the process of transition by which workers were allowed access to various fiddle benefits, therefore, were our main concerns.

What we found highlighted several points. First, it seems that the low level of pay in the hotel industry represents only one part of the total rewards available to some of its workers, since they also benefit considerably from unformalised rewards. Next, informal rewards tend to vary greatly with the bargaining power of the individual: while a group of waiters may appear to receive the same wages and do the same job, in fact some are selected for greater rewards than others because of their length of service, or the wider range of skills, abilities, experience and personal qualities which they can bring to the job. Thirdly, access to such informal rewards has become institutionalised – that is, they are accepted as a normal part of the total rewards received by a significant proportion of the workforce. Finally, one important reason for low unionisation in the industry is the greater scope for individualism which institutionalised pilferage has helped to foster.

A Starting Point

At the outset we found it useful to introduce and develop the terms Mars and Mitchell initially coined in work on the hotel and catering industry: *'ad hoc* management', 'individual contract-making', 'total rewards system' and 'core and peripheral workers'.

1 *Ad hoc management* refers to the type of crisis management required of the manager: the levels of demand for a hotel's services are unpredictable, making it difficult to develop strategies that permit a controlled response to customers' needs. An empty restaurant may fill up suddenly, or three relatively quiet nights can be followed by a fourth which strains capacity to the limit. Management has to develop *ad hoc* responses to customer demand, as against the strategic responses found throughout most of manufacturing. A traditional feature of hotel management, therefore, is that it must be flexible enough to adapt to varying demands and unanticipated crises.

2 *Individual contract-making.* To cope with this unpredictability, hotel managements have largely avoided the formal collective contract, which they regard as less effective than individual contracts made informally with their staff. When Mars was working in one restaurant he was taken aside and told his pay was being raised, 'but don't say a word about it to the others'. A week later he found that most of the others had had an increase of more than twice his amount!

Of course, the secret nature of these individual contracts makes it difficult for workers to know the proper rate for the job. But so long as the waiter *believes* that preferential treatment has been shown him by a manager, he is more likely to work at short notice or without formal payment beyond normal working hours. Indeed, it is the ambiguity surrounding people's pay, working conditions and access to informal benefits which enables management to retain control of the situation. Each member of staff in effect reaches a separate

7

agreement with his manager concerning the nature and extent of their mutual obligations.

3   *The total rewards system* is a concept which covers the *total* emoluments received by a worker, which include: basic pay; formalised perks such as subsidised food and lodging; semi-formalised perks such as tips or service charge; non-formalised additions to income from fiddles and 'knock-off' (items pilfered), together with the norms and values which determine their distribution among the workforce as a whole. It is total rewards that matter to a worker – not the level of formal pay. When an experienced waiter goes for a job he always tries to find out the *real*, the total rewards. 'What's it worth?' he will ask a confidant and will take little notice of the formal wage.

It is the ability of managements to control and manipulate the less visible and accountable aspects of the total rewards system in favour of individual workers, which has given them the autonomy they need for the smooth running of their hotels. Thus we can say that the total rewards system of the catering industry comprises BASIC PAY + SUBSIDISED LODGING + SUBSIDISED OR FREE FOOD + TIPS + 'FIDDLES' + 'KNOCK-OFFS' together with the 'climate', which offers and accepts payments in part by fiddle as normal for much of this industry.

4   *Core and peripheral workers* is a concept used to distinguish those benefiting substantially from individual contracts as against those who do not. Core workers are 'key' people whose labour is considered vital to the smooth running of the hotel or restaurant. Their speed, technical expertise, human skills, length of service and reliability distinguish them from the rest of the workforce. Although paid at the same visible rate to do the same job, the core workers' superior bargaining power gives them the ability to negotiate individual contracts providing higher informal rewards than peripheral workers normally receive. Workers in catering tend to start as peripherals and some of the less or non-stigmatised are then 'initiated' into the core.

8

The four concepts discussed here arise from the way much of this industry is structured and they go far to influence the way waiters view their world. It is an individualist's view and one which has traditionally militated against strong collectivism, as our opening quotation from Orwell (1933) has observed.

Throughout this book we explore and develop these four concepts in the light of our findings. In particular, we consider how the nature and constituents of total rewards systems vary in relation to different product and labour markets (that is, different types of hotel) and to varied patterns of ownership. We are interested in whether variations exist according to the class of hotel, the type of worker which different hotels attract, and the differences between owner-managed and conglomerate company-owned hotels. We also examine how the weightings of different parts of an individual's total rewards vary in relation to the bargaining power of each worker, and the position he holds within the organisation.

It is not our intention, however, to suggest that the four concepts which provide our starting point are only relevant to the study of hotels and restaurants. It appears, for instance, that *ad hoc management* is a feature of all industries subject to erratic demand, while the idea of *total reward systems* offers a useful way to conceptualise the complete range of benefits accruing to a job. Taken together the four concepts offer a means to focus on rewards and informal adaptations too often ignored in studies of industrial relationships and, we would suggest, are particularly appropriate to the analysis of other personal service industries. When used together with participant observation as the prime research tool, we believe that these four concepts point the way for future studies of the world of work.*

*This is a topic that has been more fully explored elsewhere – See Mars, 1982.

Planning the Study and Going to Work

THE NEED FOR DETACHMENT — AND DISCRETION

Our research strategy was based on the premise that both *involvement and detachment* are required to understand another culture. Clearly Nicod, who worked as a waiter in five different hotels, had to submerge himself entirely as a participant. But, however much care is taken, anthropologists adopting a participant-observer role will almost certainly develop blind spots. Once accustomed to the settings under investigation, there is a danger of taking for granted details which the researcher should be trying to explain. For instance, Whyte noted in his study of Chicago street gangs (1955), that everything he saw and heard was new and strange at first, but he did not have sufficient rapport with his subjects, or know enough about their world, to ask the right questions. As he became more absorbed in the local culture, the richness of the data increased and the rapport he had with those being studied improved, but he found himself becoming blind to the very behaviour that his subjects took for granted and which he was aiming to record. What concerned us, then, was how over-identification could be avoided and what safeguards we could devise against growing blind spots.

To increase the accuracy of observation and maintain objectivity, Nicod tried to disengage himself from the participant role whenever possible. Obviously, the covert stance he adopted made it impossible to record behaviour as it actually occurred, so everything he observed and was told had to be written down in private after the event. How to remember what had been said or done was not the main problem. At least Nicod did not have to contend with Ditton's dilemma of being stuck 'on the line' for twelve-hour shifts, with nowhere to go to jot things down except the lavatory cubicles. The amount of time Ditton was spending in the toilets began to get noticed. He had to pacify some genuinely concerned workmates until eventually he 'came out' as an observer — albeit in a limited way (1977, p.5). Because a waiter normally

10

works split shifts, Nicod only had to memorise details for a few hours: it was quite easy to slink off between shifts or in a slack period to scribble things down – in the seclusion of his own room, or a quiet corner of the hotel. The real danger, however, is that material gathered in this way suffers from possible selective recall. As far as possible, Nicod tried to record whole parts of conversations verbatim, and then wait until he had collected sufficient data to put an interpretation on it. To protect himself against over-identification, he limited the time spent working in each hotel, and a close and regular outside contact was maintained with Mars throughout the fieldwork. By making frequent progress reports, he became aware of omissions and explanations which were weak.

Another check came from people who were, or who had been, employed in the industry themselves, some of whom we took into our confidence about the research. (None of the names given to the characters in this book is real, and we cannot directly acknowledge the help of local informants.) In some cases, though, when it was necessary to cross-check sensitive information, the whole study might have been jeopardised if people in the field had been asked about it. Of course, this is not such a major problem when the research intent is declared. Whyte's approach, for example, in gathering material for *Street Corner Society* (1970), was to have innumerable discussions with 'Doc', one of the key informants in the group he was studying, so he could check whether he had understood the full meaning the situation had for the subjects. Nicod had to rely upon key informants outside the hotels being studied to play this kind of role – in particular Molly, the ex-waitress and friend of Mars, who gave him help in finding his first hotel.

Key informants also helped in other ways. Molly, for instance, gave Nicod a crash course in the basic skills of a waiter. He was able, then, to pose as an ex-student with some waiting experience, and gain entry as a *bona fide* waiter into the five hotels selected. The employment periods varied (the shortest was two months; the longest was five months). While at work, he watched out for 'fiddles', participating whenever necessary, but not asking too

11

many questions, and avoiding emotionally loaded topics until he had been there long enough. A sufficient degree of acceptance to enable information to be gathered, was usually achieved after about two weeks of being discreet and incurious. Not asking too many questions early on was taxing at first. But since our subjects always began to query our motives whenever we pressed them too quickly for information, the value of the less direct approach was never far from our minds.

A kitchen porter, questioned too closely shortly after Nicod began work in the second hotel, became suspicious, and asked whether the researcher was 'one of those blokes working for the government'. In the first hotel, a waitress who found him deeply engrossed in Sutherland's *The Professional Thief* (1937) while off duty, knowingly remarked, 'Now I can see why you asked me all those questions about fiddling yesterday!' The closest he came to having his cover completely blown was soon after he began work. An article appeared in the *Sunday Times* (2 August 1976) about the field research which Mars had carried out on fiddles in restaurants – only hours after he had pressed several people for information on the subject. Fortunately, the only person to notice the article was a student working in the hotel during his summer holidays and he narrowly failed to see the connection:

> It's amazing to think that we were only talking about it last night and the next thing you know, it's all over the Sunday papers.

Just as Nicod discovered the importance of not asking too many questions at first, he also learned not to over-identify with the role being played in the field* – but only after occasional errors. He felt great disappointment, for example, at not being given promotion to station head waiter, looking after his own set of tables, after working three months in his first London hotel as a commis

---

*Much has been written about the difficulties facing the participant observer in maintaining objectivity following entry into the field. In particular, Selltiz, Jahoda, Deutsch and Cook, 1969, pp. 207–21 is a useful guide. Some helpful hints are also given in Whyte, 1970, pp. 219–356. For a more psychodynamic approach on the same subject, see Gans, 1968, pp. 302–17.

(trainee waiter)! He had allowed himself to become so fully absorbed in the culture as a participant that his objectivity as an observer was impaired.

A further source of difficulty was the effect his own feelings and behaviour had on the people and events in the setting he was trying to observe. In the second hotel, for instance, he became so deeply involved in the events following a waiter's dismissal, that he assumed the role of spokesman when a confrontation developed between the restaurant manager and the waiting staff. The waiter in question had been dismissed after asking to be paid for overtime already worked. No one was a union member but it had been generally agreed to threaten strike action unless the manager agreed to the waiter's reinstatement. When the restaurant manager approached the group of waiters shortly afterwards only Nicod was prepared to speak out: 'We don't think your treatment of Francesco is reasonable.' These are hardly the words of someone maintaining an objective stance! Had the result been to precipitate actions which otherwise might not have occurred, he would have only had himself to blame. As it was, the waiter in question had already left of his own accord, saying that he would never return; and with the main cause of the dispute removed, it was decided not to strike.

The Ethics of Covert Research

There are a number of problems involved in using covert partici- pant observation as the principal research method. In particular, we had to both justify and cope with the need to fulfil covertly the researcher's role while being overtly employed as a waiter.

Because the researcher makes a conscious decision not to tell his subjects his true identity, it is argued that research of this kind is morally unacceptable: entering a group as a disguised observer is an invasion of privacy and can potentially cause discomfort to members of the group. There is also a further argument that in addition to affecting privacy, the misrepresentation involved may

13

jeopardise the anthropological profession, making it difficult to do similar research again (see Erikson, 1967).

While acknowledging some sympathy with these views, we argue that each situation varies, and indeed our adoption and defence of covert methods relate only to their use in specific conditions and for particular purposes. It was because the sensitive nature of our chosen area made it impossible to enter the field as an undisguised researcher that we decided – with some reluctance – to enter covertly. Not only would an open declaration of research intent have affected the behaviour observed, but in effect it would have limited inquiry to those who had nothing to hide or least to lose from disclosure – namely, peripheral workers who do not substantially benefit from non-taxable earnings. Our experience of overt interviewing and contact with management and staff in this industry confirmed their overall hostility to outsiders, and particularly to researchers. If we had followed the strictures of those who argue against covert methods, we would not have completed this study. In other words, we believe that the end has justified the means. How else, it has been argued, can crime be studied other than in its natural surroundings and through taking as normal a role as possible? The same applies to the study of work.

What critics of covert participant observation overlook is the peculiar restraint that a covert researcher may exercise in bringing the data to light. Indeed, we have done little or nothing to damage our subjects' personal reputations, because every effort has been made to mitigate the ethical offence. In the first place, we have omitted names and changed other irrelevant facts to protect the identity, and therefore the privacy, of those involved. We have also taken care not to report data covertly acquired wherever that publication might violate trust and cause discomfort. It can indeed be argued that far from damaging the interests of our subjects our findings might well be interpreted by them as advancing their interests. One of our informants who read an early draft of our report believed that this was in fact the case: 'It can't do anything but good to tell the truth and that's what it reads like to me.' In the final analysis, we would argue that those who adopt a covert stance are often more rigorously 'ethical' because they have a greater obligation to meet considerations of this kind than those who have declared their research intent.

GAINING AN ENTRÉE

In his search for hotels, Nicod used the same method throughout the investigation: simply tapping the widest possible sources open to anyone seeking a job in catering, namely, reading through the local press, especially the London *Evening Standard*, telephoning hotels found in the Yellow Pages or local directories, making inquiries in person off the street, applying through personal contacts and going to the hotel and catering Jobcentre in each location. This highlighted the enormous variety of ways in which one can seek employment in this industry. More significantly, though, the methods vary according to the size, type and location of hotel and the kind of worker seeking employment.

In low-level hotels, particularly those on the coast, much depends on *when* one looks for a job. First, Nicod made off-the-street inquiries in hotels along the entire length of the promenade in a northern seaside resort without receiving a single offer. When he finally did get a job, it was only after following up a number of posts advertised in the Jobcentre and local press. Yet, when he started to look for his second hotel along the promenade just two months later, he had no difficulty at all, because, with the tourist season fully under way, the demand for labour had become more acute. Less prestigious hotels tend not to have the resources to employ more staff than they actually need at any one time. In this situation the hotel manager has no choice but to accept whatever staff he can get at critical times, even if they fall below the standard he might normally expect.

When one seeks employment in the extremely prestigious hotels of London's West End, however, a different pattern emerges. Here the question of seasonal variation is not nearly so important; what matters are the skills and experience one can bring to the job. After several days spent making inquiries off the street, Nicod applied for a job advertised in the *Evening Standard* at a medium-level hotel. Because it was only a commis' job, he had no difficulty in getting it, provided he agreed to shave off his beard. But had he been seeking a higher rank or a higher-level establishment, there is little doubt that he would not have succeeded. When he did come to seek employment later on in a more prestigious establishment, he only got the job because he had been personally recommended by someone who had been employed there for fifteen years. Again, it was only a commis' job – and the restaurant manager gave him a close inspection, saying that he would have to remove his moustache and have a haircut.

Interestingly, we found that the higher the hotel's status, the less hair its waiters are allowed. Given that chefs are permitted to wear moustaches, there is no obvious reason why the same should not apply to waiters, although George Orwell has suggested the following explanation (1933):

> No one in the hotel wears a moustache, except the cooks. I should have thought you would have noticed it. Reason? There *is* no reason. It is the custom.
>
> I saw that it was an etiquette, like not wearing a white tie with a dinner-jacket, and shaved off my moustache. Afterwards I found out the explanation of the custom, which is this: waiters in good hotels do not wear moustaches, and to show their superiority, they decree that plongeurs shall not wear them either; and the cooks wear their moustaches to show their contempt for the waiters.

With his newly acquired experience at both ends of the prestige spectrum, Nicod found little difficulty in getting a job in a medium-status company-owned hotel near Cardiff. He inquired off the street about a job, and the restaurant manager asked him a number of technical questions. These included: 'What accompaniments would you serve with smoked salmon?'; 'What accompaniments would you serve with paté?' In fact, the level of expertise required was not nearly so high as one might have expected from such questions. Moreover, irrespective of the different posts people held, everyone did much the same work, despite varying skill and different wage rates. In trying to respond to varying pressures, management found it difficult to operate the bureaucratic structure the conglomerate company had sought to impose. What tended to happen was that staff were appointed at different levels but there was not really a strict differentiation of tasks — so though Nicod was employed as a chef de rang (a relatively senior waiter, usually in charge of two or more junior waiters), he did the same job as everyone else.

Appendix 1

THE FIVE HOTELS

Our sample of hotels was necessarily limited and we had to cover the broadest possible range within those limits. Table 1.1 shows the main characteristics of the five we finally selected, based on our need to reflect the factors responsible for the industry's changing staffing levels and industrial relations problems. A brief description of each of the hotels follows with charts showing their formal organisation structure.

Table 1.1   *Characteristics of the five hotels*

Hotel	Location	No of rooms	Quality rating (AA classification)	No of waiting staff
1	Northern England, coast	600	unclassified	37
2	Northern England, coast	300	☆☆☆	20
3	London, West End	40	☆☆☆☆☆	19
4	London, West End	400	☆☆☆☆☆	50
5	Cardiff	200	☆☆☆	25

17

The World of Waiters

Hotel 1: Northern England, Coast

The first hotel is a large, low-tariff conglomerate-owned hotel overlooking the sea on the coast of northern England. It is one of a small chain operating throughout London, the Midlands, the West country and the North of England. Its wide range of facilities include an indoor heated swimming pool, hairdressing salon, sauna, games room, sun lounge, nursery, television room, cocktail bar, and discothèque which stays open every night until 1 am with live and recorded music.

It had begun as an independent owner-managed hotel with a fairly good reputation for food and service. But, in trying to cope with the increasing demand from a less affluent clientele, it went the way of most large and inefficient hotels. Bankruptcy in 1973 and, not long afterwards, the loss of its three-star rating led to decline. Its immediate financial difficulties were met by a substantial local authority loan and its ownership was transferred to the company which now runs it.

One effect of the change in ownership has been the introduction of trade union representation which stands at about 50 per cent, a relatively high percentage for this industry. Yet the hotel is run with an odd combination of strong unionisation and not much team spirit. A few staff live in, but most are people from the local area who tend to keep work and non-work activity separate. In particular, a large proportion are women employed part-time or casually.

Directors periodically visit each hotel in the chain. There are four managers and three assistant managers in charge of the day-to-day running of the hotel. The restaurant manager, three head waiters and one head wine waiter have responsibility for the restaurant. There are twenty to thirty permanent fully paid waiting staff, four or five young people paid at a lower rate as commis, and ten to twenty casual staff employed to serve a single meal for banquets, normally for cash in hand. Kitchen staff have their own hierarchy: a head chef, a sous chef (who makes sauces), several chefs de partis (all-purpose chefs), commis (or trainee) chefs, as well as dishwashers and kitchen porters. In addition,

18

there is a checker whose job is to total cheques, make out bills, collect money from hotel guests and keep account of meals served.

As well as a large restaurant, there is a small grill room next to the discothèque. Service varies a great deal with seasonal demand. At the peak of the summer season each waiter might have to serve thirty to fifty people at a single sitting.

Hotel 2: Northern England, Coast

Our second hotel is in the same seaside resort; again a large low-tariff hotel, situated halfway along the promenade. Its facilities include a coffee lounge, a television lounge, ballroom, several private suites, a licensed bar, a billiards room and a cocktail bar. Its origins too lay in the golden era of hotel-keeping, but although it has a three-star rating it has long since lost the prestige it once enjoyed. To attract custom, it provides reasonably priced banqueting and conference facilities for parties ranging up to 400, and it also has its own resident band which plays at Saturday night dinner-dances.

The hotel is owned on a shareholding basis and run by directors who are among its largest shareholders. Permanent waiting staff number between ten and fifteen, but casual staff (or 'extra ducks', as they are called) are also employed whenever need arises, say, at a banquet or conference. None of the waiting staff have joined a union, despite the fact that they have a union representative – a woman employed in the linen room. Nevertheless, there is strong group solidarity: partly because of the high proportion of staff who live in (about 70 per cent), and partly because the great majority are young people who have left home and regard the hotel as a place to establish new relationships.

Matters of general policy are decided at quarterly meetings between the directors and the hotel manager. There is a general manager and an assistant manager in charge of the day-to-day running of the hotel, both men in their early and mid-twenties. The restaurant is run by the restaurant manager with the help of two head waiters – one providing general administrative assistance, the other helping more in the supervision of staff. In

19

addition, there is a head wine waiter, a receptionist in charge of totalling bills and a hierarchy of kitchen staff which is slightly more elaborate than that of the first hotel.

Hotel 3: London, West End

Nicod's third job was as a commis waiter in one of London's high-level West End establishments – a small hotel with forty bedrooms, better known as a high-quality restaurant providing late-night cabaret entertainment. Originally owned and run as a small family concern by two brothers, its heyday was the 1920s and early 1930s when it had been a High Society haunt. But during the general decline after the Second World War the two brothers sold the business to a large company which itself was taken over by a larger company in the 1950s. It is now attracting a much wider range of clientele: top businesspeople; foreign tourists; office parties, especially in the festive season; birthday parties and family celebrations in general, as well as a few regulars who have never stopped coming, and many people who simply want a night out on the town.

The restaurant employs between eighteen and twenty permanent staff, and in addition two or three casual staff are brought in on Friday and Saturday nights when trade is particularly busy. Perhaps it is a mark of prestige in our male-dominated society that its waiting staff must be men. Most of them come from Italy; some have settled in the UK, often with an Italian or English wife and children, while others, particularly the younger ones, only come to England to learn the language or to see what London has to offer. None can live in. It is against the company's policy to permit union representation among its staff. And there can hardly be an overlap between work and non-work activity when people live far from each other and do not finish work until 2 am.

Despite its relatively small size, it has a more complex management structure than the less prestigious northern hotels in which Nicod had worked. There is a general manager, a personnel manager, three trainee managers, a full-time accountant, a restaurant manager and a banqueting manager (the latter organises and supervises staff at banquets, weddings, conferences, and the like). In addition, there are five levels involved in serving food: the restaurant manager, a first head waiter, a staff head waiter, five station head waiters in charge of a set of tables and a commis waiter each. There is also a carver whose job is to carve joints of meat at lunch-time; a cashier who adds up and makes out the bills; and additional staff employed to serve drinks to the customers. Kitchen staff similarly enjoy a complex ranking in this hotel.

Hotel 4: London, West End

The fourth hotel is one of the most prestigious international hotels in London. Since the hotel was built at the turn of the century, it has enjoyed the patronage of the aristocracy and royalty, and its clientele include people from the highest levels of the business and financial world, politicians, show business personalities, leading industrialists and public figures in general. Since the Second World War, this hotel, too, has suffered a considerable fall in demand, but the management has so far resisted the idea of providing cheaper off-peak rates for party bookings. Apart from what it can earn from its bedrooms and its two restaurants it also draws a substantial part of its revenue from banquets and other grand functions.

Of the two restaurants, the one in which Nicod worked has the decor of a traditional English drawing-room: oak tables, high-quality table wear and a baronial coat of arms hanging on the wall. The other, modelled on the French style, has a dance band to provide entertainment until 1 am every morning. There are between twenty and twenty-five permanent waiting staff in each restaurant. Once again, they are exclusively male, and are drawn predominantly from Italy or Turkey, with four Turks or Turkish-Cypriots and seven Italians working in the same restaurant as Nicod. The hotel has no accommodation for staff. However, there is a relatively high proportion of union members (about 60 per cent). This is largely due to the fact that their union representative takes an active interest in union matters — and has succeeded in winning a number of concessions from management.

Perhaps not surprisingly, this hotel has the most complex organisation structure of the five. There is a general manager, an assistant manager, a personnel department, an accounts department, a 100-strong brigade of kitchen staff, floor service waiters, banqueting waiters, not to mention the fifty or so waiters who are employed in both restaurants. Within each restaurant there are further distinctions. Below the restaurant manager there is a first head waiter, a second head waiter, a third head waiter, five station head waiters, five chefs de rang and five commis waiters. Then there is a head wine waiter, two wine waiters and two commis wine waiters, as well as a carver, his chef de rang, and perhaps one or two casual staff on busy occasions.

Hotel 5: Cardiff

Our fifth hotel is a large, medium-tariff conglomerate-owned hotel in Cardiff. Its range of facilities include a guests' sitting-room, two licensed bars, two private suites for holding conferences and special functions, a cafeteria providing light snacks and cheaper meals and a restaurant offering a choice of *à la carte* and *table d'hôte* menus. Built in the late 1960s, it is primarily designed to provide a quick service for passing trade, but also enjoys the patronage of tourists, businesspeople, commercial travellers and others who need a base when spending several days in Cardiff. It also has a small number of regular customers who come for a meal on business or purely social grounds.

Waiting staff number between ten and fifteen in the restaurant and about the same again in the cafeteria. Of those who work in the restaurant only three are women, and these are fully experienced waitresses; but in the cafeteria, the waiting staff are all women, often young and inexperienced. Almost all the waiting staff live locally or live in. A social committee which comprises staff from every section within the hotel meets once a month and organise events such as staff dances, parties, football matches, basketball practice and excursions. In addition. the staff often get together informally after work, usually just for a drink before going home, but on occasion in one of the hotel's bars after normal licensing hours when someone is leaving and holding a party. In the early 1970s a number of staff had gone on strike to try to gain union recognition. They did not succeed, largely because many of the staff co-operated with the management to keep the hotel running. And although many who went on strike have subsequently been reinstated, there is still no union representation.

As one might expect, given that the hotel is part of a large bureaucratic structure, there is a highly stratified work organisation, although not on as many levels as we found in the highly prestigious London hotels. There is a general manager, an assistant manager, a personnel manager, a duty manager, three trainee managers, a kitchen staff of about fifty, plus the waiting staff in each of the two restaurants. The restaurants themselves have a ranking system which consists of restaurant manager, first head waiter, chef de rang, demi chef and commis waiter. However, the position a person holds below the rank of first head waiter is irrelevant, at least in the sense that everyone has to do the same work.

Appendix 2

FORMAL ORGANISATION: RESTAURANT STRUCTURES IN THE FIVE HOTELS

Key:

D	= Director	B	= Bar worker
M	= Manager	1HWW	= First head wine waiter
AM	= Assistant manager	1HW	= First head waiter
RM	= Restaurant manager	2HW	= Second head waiter
HWW	= Head wine waiter	CR	= Chef de rang
CH	= Checker/cashier	DC	= Demi chef
HW	= Head waiter	CW	= Commis waiter
SHW	= Station head waiter	CWW	= Commis wine waiter
WW	= Wine waiter	BM	= Banqueting manager
DW	= Dish washer	BW	= Banqueting waiter
		W	= Cafeteria waiter

(The number following a symbol denotes how many actually hold that position.)

Hotel 1

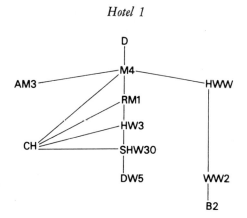

Hotel 2

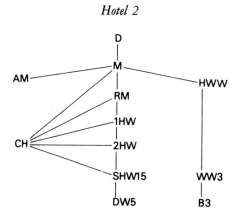

24

Hotel 3

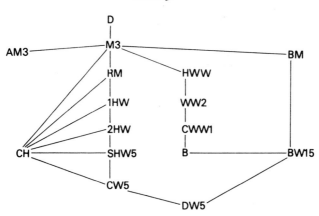

Hotel 4

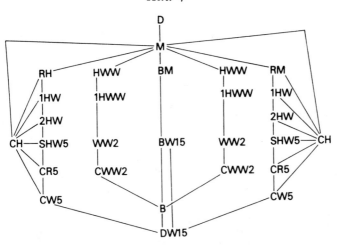

25

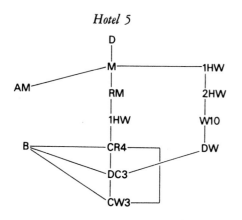

Hotel 5

2

What Is Service?:
Giving That Little Extra

The Idea of Service

> Mr Sathe, an accountant from Mysore, said: 'I had taken my wife to
> the Vignyana Bharati restaurant for our wedding anniversary
> supper. When the idli was served she noticed it contained a
> cockroach. She called my attention to the cockroach and I called
> the waiter. The waiter picked up the cockroach and, greatly to our
> surprise, popped it into his mouth, saying: 'This is a delicious
> onion, not a cockroach.'
>
> Asked why he had promoted the waiter to headwaiter after a trial
> of only three weeks, Mr Urs, the restaurant's owner, said: 'He is a
> man who may well give many years of good service.'
>
> ('True Stories', *Private Eye*, 6 June 1980)

Perhaps the most significant of the many changes that have
occurred in the hotel and catering industry since the Second World
War has been the development of wider facilities to meet different
markets and types of clientele. There are still a small number of
highly prestigious top international-class hotels, such as Clar-
idge's, the Savoy, the Ritz and the Dorchester. But there is an
increasing number of establishments aimed at the lower end of the
market: cheap hotels, motels, holiday camps, guest houses,
boarding houses, hostels and the like. And the number of mod-
erately priced eating places has also greatly increased since the
1960s: ethnic restaurants, snack bars, wine bars, take-away food
outlets and self-service restaurants now exist in vast numbers.

Much of what we have to say about service in hotel restaurants applies equally to these places.

We are therefore discussing an industry which includes widely differing organisations serving very diverse markets. We have chosen to treat hotels as a single industry with different sectors having different problems, because variations between hotels are less obvious than the characteristics they hold in common: *whatever* else a hotel and especially its restaurant aims to do, it must always provide *service*. Just what it is that people are supposed to be serving or receiving varies in different parts of the industry, but some notions about service are widely applicable so that our first concern is to find a definition of 'ideal' service and then to see how this applies at both ends of the prestige spectrum.

Different meanings attach to the term 'service'; we are not simply referring to the serving of food. Service involves the need to supply customer satisfaction in a variety of ways, not all of which are explicit or easy to define: often service is judged on the most intangible aspects of customer satisfaction, especially in highly prestigious hotels and restaurants. A satisfactory definition must be relevant to the whole industry, and refer to the total actions and physical features, beyond a bare minimum. Thus 'service' as we use it, refers to an action or material thing that is more than one might normally expect. In a transport cafe it can mean no more than passing the sauce bottle with a smile. In the Savoy it might mean making prodigious efforts to supply a rare delicacy or indulging a customer's particular preference or foible.

The more people actually pay for service, the more exacting will be their demands for better *and more individual* service. As we move down the scale towards mass catering, people become less demanding. The extent to which the service ideal and its practical fulfilment coincides varies. Broadly, the match between the ideal (expectations) and the norm (what actually happens) is enormously close at the top and bottom of the market. The interesting discrepancies occur in the middle area which is expanding and where ambiguity prevails. Here, as we shall see, customers' expectations are uncertain and managements are at their weakest

28

in dealing with the essentially erratic nature of the demand for their product. The concepts of service at each end of the spectrum can be broadly termed 'individual' and 'mass'.

In the hotels where satisfaction of a customer's individual needs has highest priority, one expects, and finds, the emphasis on personal choice and quality. Here complaints are treated very seriously. All such hotels have a number of defining characteristics in common. In the restaurants, these include a wide choice in both *à la carte* and *table d'hôte* menus, less emphasis on quantity and more on quality, a greater scope for the customer to set the pace, few restrictions on personal space (that is, plenty of elbow-room and space between tables), high-quality tableware and highly skilled and specialised staff. The ability to provide such service depends on having a high staff/customer ratio, a low turnover of production, relatively large units of profit, slow returns on outlay and low staff turnover rates, especially among its skilled labour. Tables 2.1 and 2.2 show how the two high-level London hotels we studied follow this pattern.

Now if we turn to the other end of the spectrum, we find the antithesis of everything mentioned so far. Most forms of mass catering (industrial canteens, self-service, take-away, and the like) thrive by trying to meet demand for a cheaper product with only the thinnest layer of service. Most people have a fairly clear idea of the features that characterise such establishments: a limited choice of menu; more emphasis on quantity and less on quality; the customer has little opportunity to set the pace; limited access to tables and chairs, often making it necessary to share a table with strangers; cheap plastic cups and plates; an absence of fabric table covers; and inexperienced, semi-skilled and unskilled staff. Certainly, in the northern hotels we studied, the emphasis was on having to reduce production costs through labour cuts and lower quality of output. There was a low staff/customer ratio, a high turnover of production, relatively small unit profits, quick returns on outlay and high labour turnover rates, at least among peripheral workers (see Tables 2.3 and 2.4).

On the whole, people who use the 'mass' establishments know

29

Table 2.1 *Conglomerate ownership, metropolitan, 40 bedrooms, one restaurant with a maximum seating capacity of 120: Hotel 3*

No of customers allocated to each waiter on average sitting	12
Average length of customers' sitting time	1 hr 30 mins (lunch) 3 hrs (dinner/cabaret)
Cost of average meal (wine included)	10X (lunch) 15X (dinner)
Average gross weekly earnings of waiter	50X (incl. tips) + service

N.B.   Prices and earnings are quoted in X for comparison.

Table 2.2 *Non-conglomerate ownership, metropolitan, 400 bedrooms, two restaurants with a maximum seating capacity of 150 each: Hotel 4*

No of customers allocated to each waiter on average sitting	8
Average length of customers' sitting time	1 hr 30 mins
Cost of average meal (wine included)	15X
Average gross weekly earnings of waiters	60X (incl. tips)

N.B.   Prices and earnings are quoted in X for comparison.

that they are paying little, they do not expect too much, and they are usually not disappointed. The hotels and restaurants competing at this level offer roughly the same standard of food and service and complaints tend to be few. When a complaint is received it might well be casually dismissed or treated in a cavalier manner. One customer at a self-service counter, who had protested at the limited range on offer and who asked if that was the only choice, was told: 'No – there's another – you can take it or leave it!' Another who complained about a dirty knife was advised to 'try the Savoy, sir.'

Between these two extremes is the expanding middle area: that part of the industry dominated by big hotels in city areas, largely

Table 2.3 *Conglomerate ownership, seaside, 600 bedrooms, one restaurant with a maximum seating capacity of 600, drill room seating 50 (mainly used by non-residents): Hotel 1*

No of customers allocated to each waiter on average sitting	30
Average length of customers' sitting time	45 mins
Cost of the average meal (wine included)	2.5X
Average gross weekly earnings of waiter	40X (incl. tips)

N.B. Prices and earnings are quoted in X for comparison.

Table 2.4 *Non-conglomerate ownership, seaside, 300 bedrooms, one restaurant with a maximum seating capacity of 200, grill room seating 20 (mainly used by non-residents): Hotel 2*

No of customers allocated to each waiter on average sitting	25
Average length of customers' sitting time	60 mins
Cost of the average meal (Wine included)	4X
Average gross weekly earnings of waiter	30X (incl. tips)

N.B. Prices and earnings are quoted in X for comparison.

built since the late 1960s and belonging to a small number of conglomerate companies. Some newly built hotels offer a new product or service, such as being conveniently situated near an airport. Others have more in common with the older traditional hotels. However, the ideology and business orientation of their senior managers especially, derived as they often are from outside the industry, tend to be different from those of traditional hotel owners and managers and are subject to constraints of a very different kind.

The danger for these medium-level hotels is that they are likely to fall victim to their own competitive advertising and marketing policies. As a result they are often judged on the same criteria as those hotels higher up the hierarchy, when, in fact, they possess many of the characteristics and problems of those lower down: they operate in a more competitive market, have higher turnover of production, lower staff/customer ratios and relatively small unit costs. For these reasons there is often a gap between customers' expectations and the reality of what can be offered relative to the prices charged. There is thus a grey ambiguous area that is the source of much dissatisfaction. The medium-level Cardiff hotel we studied provides a good example of what we call this 'ambiguous middle' range (see Table 2.5). Complaints here sometimes appear ludicrous when assessed against price. One woman, for instance, was appalled to find that the salmon in a cheap cucumber and salmon sandwich came from a tin, when she had been reassured that it was not only fresh, but had been rushed from Scotland!

ELASTICITY OF DEMAND

We propose two hypotheses for predicting the kind of service likely to be judged as good. In high-prestige hotels where food and service are expensive, a rise in price will not be accompanied by a proportionate decline in sales. In such hotels running costs will always be high because of the large numbers of highly skilled staff needed to meet the demand for individual service. Any increase in the cost of production will be passed directly to the consumer who will have to pay more. But the demand for this kind of service is inelastic: as long as there are people willing to pay for the best that money can buy, there will always be a steady demand for it, hardly responsive to price changes. Thus, in the prestigious hotels we have described, people are more inclined to disregard relative prices when choosing from the menu.

Of course, this is not always the case: for example, a customer who only ordered an omelette in our highest level London hotel apologised to the waiter for not having ordered more, explaining that he had chosen the least expensive item on the menu since all he

Table 2.5   *Conglomerate ownership, medium urban, 200 bedrooms, one restaurant with a maximum seating capacity of 200, grill room seating 200: Hotel 5*

No of customers allocated to each waiter on average sitting	25
Average length of customers' sitting time	1 hr 25 mins
Cost of the average meal (wine included)	6X
Average gross weekly earnings of waiter	45X (incl. tips)

N.B.   Prices and earnings are quoted in X for comparison.

wanted was to be able to say he had eaten in this luxury restaurant. But, given that the normal demand for expensive, high-quality food and service comes from the well-to-do, the demand for individual service remains steady, however high the price.

In mass catering the reverse applies. Here elasticity of demand in relation to price changes will be high: any rise in price will normally be followed by a greater-than-proportionate decline in sales. Because competition is high, increases in costs of production have to be met as far as possible without raising the price for the consumer. Low staffing and poor-quality food may help to keep costs down but, as even the slightest rise in consumer prices may bring a disproportionate decline in sales, practically nothing can be done to maintain the balance. Greater competition means that people simply take their custom elsewhere whenever they see the opportunity to pay less. In such hotels increased running costs, therefore, have to be met by whatever means are judged likely to have the least impact on consumer demand.

It is between these two extremes that we find the discrepancies between expectations and reality mentioned earlier – this is the realm of the ambiguous middle. High expectations tend not to be fulfilled, basically because low staffing and poor quality food militate against the service ideal. On the other hand, among those who use this middle range are large numbers of people for whom quality is not so important, and whose interest lies more in keeping down price. The problem for these hotels is that little can be done to reduce costs because of the high expectations of a significant number of customers but at the same time overall elasticity of demand will be high.

ROUTINE VERSUS EMERGENCY

Closely connected with the capacity to fulfil the expectations of customers is Hughes' distinction between routine and emergency (1958, pp. 54–5). Hughes noted that in many cases those who have need of a service perceive it as something of an emergency. For them, after all, it tends to be a one-off event. Those providing the service, however, deal with the matter routinely. For them, one act of service is much like another. Hughes suggests that this distinction is a source of chronic tension.

This dilemma is most marked in highly prestigious hotels where customers expect a strong element of personal service. Should a waiter fail to pay sufficient attention to their needs, they often feel he is trying to belittle their importance; he is not taking the job – or them – seriously enough. The waiter's very competence, however, comes from having served exactly the same order to a thousand previous customers, each of whom would like to think that the culinary experience was uniquely his or hers.

The customers with particularly high expectations are obvious to the waiter and he develops strategies for supplying satisfaction and defusing complaints. The station head waiter may, for example, enact a charade of publicly dressing down his staff for the benefit of a complaining customer. Or he may prefer to go to the kitchen himself and place or receive an order for an awkward customer, rather than leave it to his commis. At one of the most prestigious London hotels we studied, one station head waiter always went to the kitchen himself to ask for extra chives in the vichyssoise soup whenever he served a particular customer: 'He's a real bastard; if he thinks there aren't enough, he's bound to kick up a fuss.'

In the minds of those receiving the service, then, there is always the possibility of resentment that something so special to them can be treated so routinely by those who provide it, even though it is obvious that such an attitude implies competence, and any sign of incompetence would not be tolerated. To sum up: 'his emergency is my routine', which is why the art of service often lies in creating an impression that there is something of a struggle involved in supplying satisfaction.

By contrast, in less prestigious hotels, the very opposite tends to be the case. Waiters have to develop emergency tactics to give the impression that everything is going according to plan. Because the waiter is attending to large numbers of people at the same time, the problem is not so much that he may belittle the importance of those he serves; it is more a question of trying not to fall short of certain minimum standards that customers normally expect. Here, again, the experienced waiter seeking to supply satisfaction and defuse complaints has to develop strategies to deal with the customer and anticipate problems that so often arise. But the impression he hopes to give has little to do with engendering the belief that his relationship has something special or unique about it; instead he hopes to suggest that there is nothing extraordinary about his routine. Thus, if something about his performance suggests he is having to struggle to maintain control, he must show this is not normal and should simply be regarded as the best he can do in abnormal circumstances. In brief, he seeks to give the impression of having everything under control when, in fact, he is probably having a struggle to cope: 'his routine is my emergency', and the service ideal implies being able to tackle the unanticipated crises that arise without showing signs of excitement or panic.

The Waiter/Customer Relationship

Whatever the level of hotel, waiters must always aim to meet the expectations of their customers. They do this by offering an idealised view of their situation, which involves concealing or

35

underplaying activities, facts and motives which are incompatible with the impression they are attempting to put over. They are actors putting on a performance, but the need to disguise the discrepancy between what the audience expects and what it gets varies along the prestige scale.

Most of the waiters in the highly prestigious hotels where Nicod worked said they thought that to succeed in their profession they needed to be pleasant, charming, polite and discreet. Others emphasised the need to show respect and play a submissive role. Interestingly enough, however, few were prepared to put technical expertise or knowledge high on their list although, when asked, most said these were extremely important.

> In order to please you have to be charming. Just look at me for instance. I know I don't speak English very well, so when it comes to describing what dishes are on the menu I'm not very good. But everyone will tell you I'm very good at putting on the charm. It helps me a lot to keep people happy, even if they're not too pleased with the food or service otherwise. It also helps if I'm dealing with people in a tricky situation such as having to ask them to leave because they're not suitably dressed. (Station head waiter, Hotel 3)

> It doesn't take a good head on your shoulders to be a good waiter. All you really need in this business to get on is the ability to say 'Yes Sir, No Sir, Three Bags Full Sir'. If you can do nothing else, it doesn't matter so long as you can keep this up. (Station head waiter, Hotel 4)

Customer satisfaction is not determined by the food alone and, however extraordinary or awkward their requests, most customers can get whatever they want, provided they pay for it. A retired colonel, a regular customer in Hotel 3, who invariably asked for poached turbot whenever he came for lunch took everyone by surprise on one occasion with a request for 'bacon, bangers and mash'. This did not even appear on the menu, being the kind of dish not generally served in a high-class establishment. Although it was much cheaper to prepare than dishes on the menu, it was charged to the customer at the full *table d'hôte* rate. Had it not been for other aspects of the service – the personal element, greater privacy, better decor, expensive tableware, and so on – the customer might have gone elsewhere and had the same meal for less than half the price.

Then there is the case of a customer in Hotel 4 who ordered two bananas for dessert. Like all raw fruit, the bananas were served on a silver platter with a knife ready for the customer to peel them herself; and the price was high. The customer called for a waiter and asked him to peel them for her. As a general rule a waiter should not be seen to touch food, so he set about the task just as if he were carving a joint of meat. With a carving knife in one hand and a fork in the other, he carefully cut along both edges of the skin until nothing but the bare inside was left for the customer to eat. Here, again, the personal element of service supersedes everything else. Ideally a customer has only to begin to look around in a top class restaurant and a waiter should glide over to ask what he would like. Because the waiting staff know what is normally expected and because management generally have sufficient resources to meet the most idiosyncratic demands, there is no great disparity between the service ideal and its practical fulfilment.

Oddly enough, the same appears true of hotels at the other end of the prestige spectrum. Here, a large number of customers are 'passing trade' whose main concern is to obtain cheap and quick service before they move on to their next port of call; or they are seeking cheap holiday accommodation for short periods. So long as the hotel satisfies their basic requirements, such people rarely complain: they get what they pay for and do not expect more. Thus in the northern hotels we studied, people's complaints never focused upon the quality of service, but tended to be about the speed of service. It is assumed that whatever people pay, there is no excuse for slow service, and jokes frequently drive the point home.

Diner: 'Are you the waiter I gave my order to? I expected an older man.' (*Gloucester Citizen*)

Here the low expectations of customers can easily be met; and where there is a gap at this level between what people expect and the service they receive, it is usually because management has insufficient resources to cope with the demand.

THE PROBLEMS OF THE AMBIGUOUS MIDDLE

Between these two extremes is the expanding middle area where ambiguity prevails. Here customers' expectations are uncertain because hotels have neither clearly defined 'mass' nor clearly defined 'individual' traits. On the one hand, some customers may be disappointed because they expect the kind of service normally associated with less prestigious hotels. A customer in our medium-status conglomerate hotel in Cardiff complained because she preferred to fetch her own coffee from a machine (a practice at another hotel she had stayed in) rather than be served by a waiter at her table: her reason was that people get to know one another better because they begin to strike up a conversation while they wait in the queue. This might well be true, but for a hotel seeking to model itself on the high-level type of establishment, or at least to project such an image, it runs counter to the very notion of service.

On the other hand, some customers may be disappointed not to receive the kind of service they associate with high-level establishments. Here where waiters are overstretched, as they take an order, they tend to fidget, impatiently poised – like an athlete on a standing start – always ready to sprint off to another table. Here too, 'waiter's eye' is a chronic condition and catching it from the customer's viewpoint often provides an exercise in exasperation. A complaining diner, who was dissatisfied with the service he received in a Jewish restaurant in Jerusalem, commented to the waiter: 'It's easy to see you've never been a waiter at the London Ritz.' ('It's easy to see you've never been a *guest* at the London Ritz,' the waiter replied.) (Mikes, 1950.) The danger for all hotels of medium status is of customers' expectations being raised so high that they cannot actually be met.

Obviously, at all points along the prestige spectrum, discrepancies are likely between the ideal and the norm, but nowhere is this

38

more marked than in the medium-status hotel. Here strategies enabling a better showing to be made are integral to the performance that is put on and sustained. This is illustrated by the drastic lengths to which a waiter may often have to go to confirm his customer's image and maintain standards.

At 'Shetland Hotel', a family tourist hotel on the island of Shetland, Goffman (1959a, pp. 84, 118–20) recorded an overall impression of middle-class service projected by the owner-managers whenever guests were present. They presented themselves in the roles of middle-class host and hostess, and their employees as domestics. In fact, in terms of the local class structure, the girls who acted as maids were of slightly higher status than their employers. When hotel guests were absent, the owners and employees spent a considerable amount of time together with no pretence of any status differences. This intimacy and equality between management and staff was inconsistent with the guests' notions of the social distance that ought to obtain between them, just as it was inconsistent with the impression both fostered when guests were present, but this teamwork ensured a good staff showing.

Creating the Right Impression

Nicod witnessed many subterfuges involved in fostering the right impression, and again these were particularly a feature of 'the ambiguous middle.'* First of all, much time and effort is usually required well before a waiter can actually provide the food. When little effort is expended to prepare the food and, for example, frozen foods or microwave ovens are used, this fact will be concealed. If those who serve in the restaurant are to maintain an impression of high quality, they must conceal what the kitchen staff really do and try to sustain the customers' image of a kitchen

---

*In presenting this material we owe much to Goffman's analysis of the way in which people generally behave, in particular how they foster an idealised impression of their routine. See Goffman, 1959a, esp. pp. 44–59.

full of people feverishly preparing the food. Or the opposite may be the case, and it will be the considerable effort behind the service that will be hidden. For example, the nonchalant air affected by many waiters and waitresses contrasts with the anger and frustrations they so often display when queuing in the kitchen for food. One solution is for waiting staff to work in co-operative pairs, but in lower-level hotels (where individual entrepreneuriality is more pronounced) they often prefer to work on their own, using a system of placing trays to mark their position in the queue. This allows the waiters to take orders or serve *hors d'oeuvre*, sweets and coffee rather than waste time waiting for a main course.

A second source of irritation that waiters may have to conceal from customers is the chronic shortage of materials, such as china and cutlery, that so often exists. A surprisingly high proportion of all the arguments and fights that take place between staff are connected with the struggle to get enough china and cutlery to lay their tables. Out of despair, some resort to taking things from others when they are not looking. Accusations abound and ill feelings run deep, especially if supplies run short just as waiters are beginning to re-lay their tables for more customers in the same sitting. And when some waiters are hoarding large supplies of cutlery and china ready for use when required, the effect is to reduce the total available stock, making it harder still to find supplies. Of course the fastest service is generally provided by those who have spent the greatest time and effort in hoarding materials. In her study of Manchester restaurants, Bowey (1976, p. 140) noted that waitresses would hoard materials in a little cupboard, called a 'dumb waiter', from which they served their tables. But Nicod found a wider variety of private storage places: on the floor below side-tables, behind the curtains next to the window, beneath a piano on the stage, in the staff cloakroom, in shopping bags, cardboard boxes, coat pockets, and so on. Some even took materials home for safekeeping, while others kept theirs firmly under lock and key.

Then there is the fact that waiters tend to hide any evidence of tasks which embody Hughes' notion of 'dirty work' (1958, pp.

40

49–53), which is present in some form in all occupations. Dirty work may involve tasks which are physically unclean, semi-legal, cruel, or degrading in various ways, but these disturbing facts are seldom expressed or fully declared unless they are an integral part of the very activity which gives the occupation its charisma. In the case of a physician, for instance, whose hands are 'dirty' from having to handle the human body, this part of his work is integrated into the role he plays. The waiter, however, is more like the janitor whose job is to handle other people's rubbish. It involves having to lay tables, fetch and carry food, clear away dirty dishes and throw away half-eaten food. For him the most satisfying and prestige-giving part of the job – and the activity on which he is mainly judged by others – is serving the food. Dirty work, therefore, is not knit into some satisfying and prestige-giving definition of his role, but is rather something imposed on him which he tries to brush aside or delegate to others if possible.

In highly prestigious hotels, the different ranks are integrally connected to the relative cleanliness of the functions they perform. Those who have risen to the rank of station head waiter delegate the more lowly of their tasks to others. Those at the top of the hierarchy have something of the surgeon's status. They are the ones who perform the miracle and their dirty work is done by others. By contrast, those who perform the dirty work (that is, nursing staff in the first case, or the chefs de rang and commis waiters in the second) fare badly in the prestige ratings, not being among the miracle-workers and only able to operate at the margins.

In lower-level hotels, however, the division of labour is not so marked, and the theme of uncleanliness has little to do with rankings. Here it is the waiter's role to perform both the prestige-bearing and the less satisfying part of the job himself because little or none of the dirty work can be delegated. No wonder his professional status is so low, when he has to conceal so much of what he actually does from those he serves (see Hughes, 1958, pp. 72–3).

Closely connected with the notion of dirty work is a fourth discrepancy – that between the appearance and the actual reality of a service. Since the notion of service embodies several ideal standards, a good showing means it is likely that some standards will only be sustained in public by the sacrifice of some of the others in private. What tends to happen is that, if there are standards whose loss can be concealed, waiters will sacrifice them to maintain those standards which are most visible. Thus if service is judged on the basis of speed and quality, quality will fall before speed because it is usually possible to conceal poor quality, but slow service is obvious.

Whenever staff ran short of ground coffee in Hotel 3, they would serve instant coffee instead because, in the restaurant manager's words, 'By the time they're ready for coffee, they're usually too pissed to notice the difference.' Similarly, when a lot of coffee was needed in Hotel 5, a waitress taught Nicod how to save time by making two pots of coffee out of one: 'Just make a normal pot to begin with, pour half of it into a second pot, and then add boiling water to both of them. They won't mind, they don't like it too strong.' Another similar trick Nicod picked up in Hotel 3 was to mix the mustard together whenever supplies of one particular variety ran short. Although French 'Dijon' and English mustard have their own distinctive flavours, both are a similar yellowish-brown colour and when mixed in equal quantities cannot easily be distinguished from one another, either by colour or by taste. 'It'll take a good one to tell the difference – and not one in fifty's that good!' was how one waiter put it.

So, too, if those serving find it difficult to provide quick service and maintain standards of hygiene, it is poor hygiene which can be readily concealed. Many examples arise; for instance, reusing unwashed dishes, using spittle to clean cutlery, wiping china and cutlery with a serving cloth that is dirty through over-use, handling food to test how hot it is, and so on.

Finally, when the discrepancy between actual activity and the impression the waiter is seeking to foster becomes so great that he can no longer keep up the pretence, there is nothing he can do but play his last card. In one of our northern hotels, where an acute shortage of milk jugs frequently posed a problem for waiting staff, it was common practice for milk to be served in tea pots, coffee pots, water jugs, beer mugs and a wide variety of other such vessels, ready to hand and adapted for the purpose. In this kind of case it is simply not possible to practise concealment because nothing can be done to hide the fact that something is wrong, and waiters cannot try to pass off what is happening as somehow unusual. If all else fails, they have little choice but to appeal to the customer's goodwill and persuade him that difficulties have arisen due to circumstances beyond their control; that it is a unique situation, and will not happen again.

This strategy can only be effective in dealing with passing trade who know nothing about the real situation; but, in any case, it is a last-ditch measure, a step taken only when all else fails. Its danger is that it must not be used too often or with regulars or residents. One restaurant manager who had to work with a perpetual shortage of equipment explained:

> 'We always had the Dickens of a job trying to persuade people that this was not the way we usually treated our customers. . . that the service was usually much better. But one day we had a crusty colonel-type – a regular – and he was served by a new waiter who snivelled on with our usual sob story about why on that occasion we had no ice for the ice-bucket. This fellow just blew "his top" and he shouted out at the top of his voice: "Don't give me that crap again! The last three times I've been here you've come out with the same bloody story."'

The Waiter/Chef Relationship

So far we have been considering the idea of service from the viewpoint of the waiter and seeing how this colours his interactions with customers. After all, it is the essential contact between server and served that is basic to any service occupation. But in nearly all such occupations the server is not alone: he depends upon the involvement of a back-up team. In the hotel industry, it is this dimension that can make the difference between good and bad service. So when we talk about service in

43

this industry, we cannot ignore the vital link between waiter and chef.

A problem for the waiter is having to depend upon the chef for the basic material of his craft – the food. Although waiters tend to be judged in terms of the total satisfaction that they are able to provide, sometimes they are judged simply by the quality of food they serve – even though they have had no part in its preparation or cooking. Much of the tensions that arise between waiter and chef stem from this identification of the waiter with the food he serves. In applying pressure on the kitchen staff (largely through shouting abuse and insults), waiters hope to establish some control over the quality and the speed of service, and over their own routine and the performance they put on in front of their customers.

Often, though, whatever the reasons given by customers for their dissatisfaction, it is not so much the quality of the food as other aspects of service that really matter to them. These are: speed, technical waiter skills, and some indefinable social skill which customers have come to expect. So when customers claim that something is wrong with the food, the quality of the food is not necessarily their main complaint: it might be the easiest way to express their dissatisfaction about the service in these terms. After all it takes less courage to blame the absent chefs.

Here there is a good case for saying that the division of labour is more than functional; that there are infinite social-psychological nuances in it (Hughes, 1958, pp. 72–7). As one highly experienced and much travelled waitress put it: 'You don't often find cats and dogs being friendly now do you? It's not in their nature. And that's how it is between the kitchen and the dining room – and it's the same all over the world.' Thus the chef-waiter conflict is not just an expression of the status inconsistencies between them, but arises from more fundamental differences in their objectives. And it is always present – ready to be triggered whenever the waiter finds himself held to blame for the poor craftsmanship of the chef, or whenever the chef is held to blame for the incompetence of the waiter.

In explaining this conflict which so frequently arises between those who cook and those who serve, Whyte has suggested that waiting staff have no other way of 'letting off steam' and so divert the pressure under which they work on to the only available target. He also suggested that, when kitchen staff are men and the waiting staff women, the potential conflict is more intense than when both are female or both male, because men find it difficult if women initiate action for them (1948, p. 64). Bowey contends that male chefs conflict with waiters just as often as with waitresses, and she has developed a different interpretation of male-female relationships (1976, pp. 36–7).

> Since men in the restaurant industry . . . are more career-orientated than women . . . it follows that they will be more strongly motivated towards achieving objectives related to their careers than will women . . . One of these career-related objectives is the achievement of high quality in the food they prepare. Since this objective brings the chef into conflict with the waiting staff, we would expect to find conflict between chefs and waitresses occurring more intensively and more frequently than between female kitchen staff and waitresses.

While it is true that an unpleasant encounter with a customer may cause a waiter to snap at the next person he meets – usually one of the kitchen staff – we think this is not the main cause of dispute. Like Bowey, we found as much intense conflict between chefs and waiters as between chefs and waitresses. On the other hand, if Bowey is correct, we might expect that the more waiters or waitresses have to depend upon career-oriented chefs, the more likely it is they will conflict with them. From Nicod's experience in two of the most prestigious hotels in London, however, this certainly was not the case. For one thing, the food was of better quality so that the customers were less likely to complain. Rows were always more frequent – and more dramatic – in the less prestigious northern hotels studied, where those who prepared meals were men, but not so strongly career-oriented as those in London.

But a further reason can be adduced for the lower level of

complaints in high-prestige hotels: waiters are not so pressed for time by their customers. The more sophisticated the customers, the more they will recognise that high quality food preparation always takes time – a factor that contributes to the extra individuality of the service. And if they appear unaware of this, it can always be tactfully pointed out to them. But it can usually be assumed that such customers can afford to spend their time like they spend their money – liberally.

A final reason for the reduced conflict in high-prestige hotels has to do with the waiters' system of ranking. In a high-level hotel, those who serve the food rank highest of all – and they delegate their 'dirty work' to the chefs de rang or commis waiters who work under them. This rigid division of labour means that chefs and waiting staff avoid one another at the higher levels. Only the commis waiter normally comes into direct contact with the kitchen staff – and in dealing with, say, the chef or the sous chef, he must always be ready to show as much deference as befits someone of higher rank in the kitchen. If he fails to do so, he may upset the delicate balance which operates there. Soon after Nicod began work as a commis in Hotel 4, for example, he came perilously close to this. The sous chef, the middle-level kitchen ranker, half jokingly and half seriously, commented because he had not been addressed in a proper manner:

> What, just a commis, and you've got the cheek to call me Nobby? You'll have to learn a few manners before you give me the next order, boy. My name, as far as you're concerned, is *Mr* Nobby!

By contrast, in a lower-level hotel such delegation is possible only to a limited extent: rigidly defined roles and ranks do not as a rule exist, and it is not possible to insulate those who prepare and cook from those who serve. Every waiter or waitress must come into direct contact across the serving counter with the kitchen staff. And it is in low-level hotels that both kitchen and waiting staff are most often the victims of customers' complaints because of other people's errors. They are the very source of each other's problems, and there is no barrier between them to prevent conflict.

46

We conclude that to understand conflict between waiters and chefs one element matters more than anything else: this is the class of hotel – not the sex or career motivation of those involved. In hotels at the lower end of the spectrum, we find conflict between those who prepare and cook and those who serve; any aspirations the chef might have concerning quality run directly counter to the waiter's concern with speed. But as we move up the hierarchy there is not such a conflict of interests. Here the chef's concern is likewise with quality, but he is not under pressure from the waiter for faster service, because the waiter's concern is with quality too.

How 'Grand' is a Hotel? The Relationship between Service and Status

We have so far focused on the concept of service because this is the key trait that all hotels (and restaurants) can be said to have in common. If we take the analysis further, there are still problems of definition and classification. Whenever things are classified together because they have one dominant characteristic in common, we assume that they also share other secondary characteristics. We accept that there are several dominant characteristics forming the basis of a classification of hotels, one of which is the kind of service they provide. Here service is related to the defining characteristics of two grand categories of hotel, mass versus individualistic, and in this respect it is distinguished from a classification based upon the hotel's status.

Master and Auxiliary Status Traits

We make use of Hughes' (1945) distinction between master and auxiliary traits to help us to categorise hotels. Hughes notes that most statuses have one key trait which serves to distinguish those who belong from those who do not. It might, for example, be the formal or legal requirements a person must fulfil to enter a given

47

profession. Thus, whatever else he may be, the doctor is a person who has a certificate stating that he has passed the prescribed examinations and is licensed to practise medicine. There might, on the other hand, be no formal or legal qualifications for membership, but instead all those who belong are informally expected to possess a master trait. For example, there might be no formal or legal requirement for a person to call himself a supporter of a political party but he would at least be informally expected to vote in support of that party at an election.

However, as Hughes points out, in addition to having a master trait, people often have auxiliary characteristics determining their status relative to one another. Thus many people in our society also expect a doctor to be respectably middle class, heterosexual, restrainedly polite and possibly white, male and Protestant. It follows that one may have formal qualifications for entry to a status but be denied full acknowledgement because of a lack of the proper auxiliary traits: one may, for instance, be a doctor but be ebullient, female, black, dissolute or have a propensity to dress in beach wear at the surgery.

Hughes deals with this phenomenon in regard to statuses that are thought of as desired and desirable. But the same process occurs in statuses that are deviant or not so desirable (Becker, 1963, pp. 32–9). To be labelled a deviant may carry connotations specifying the traits associated with anyone bearing the label. Thus a man known to have committed an offence is not only labelled a criminal. He is also presumed likely to commit similar offences again and, because he has shown himself 'without respect for the law', may be considered likely to commit entirely different crimes as well. In short, what Becker is saying is that apprehension for one deviant act is all that is necessary to be labelled deviant: this is the master trait. And because he possesses one deviant master trait, a person is assumed also to possess other deviant traits; that is, the auxiliary traits allegedly associated with it.

Both Hughes and Becker were concerned to analyse the statuses of individuals. But there is no reason why the same concept cannot be applied to the collective statuses associated with a work-group or an organisation. As with individuals, some traits, the 'master traits', assume priority over others in defining the status of a work-group or organisation. In hotels this is the kind of service they provide. To treat a hotel as though it possesses high or low status presupposes a certain kind of service appropriate to all hotels of the same kind. It brings to people's minds an image of what they expect hotels of this kind to be like. To be sure, initial expectations may be set by price levels alone but judgement – confirmation of the image – depends upon more than price.

How hotels are judged, then, depends on their capacity to match the image people have of them, using a variety of criteria derived from other similar hotels as a yardstick. The fact that a hotel has high-quality food, good decor, expensive tableware and plenty of elbow-room will not prevent it being regarded as low status if it fails to provide individualistic service. On the other hand, people are surprised and find it anomalous if a hotel has the kind of service they expect but lacks other traits characteristically associated with hotels of its kind. Thus we might find a hotel offering expensive and individual service but poor food, or unattractive decor and tableware. It will therefore fail to qualify as a high-level establishment. Table 2.6 summarises the traits associated with hotels at each end of the spectrum.

Table 2.6   *Status-Defining Features of a Hotel*

Master trait	Auxiliary traits			
Kind of service	Food	Time	Space	
Individualistic	High quality; wide choice, good presentation	Customers able to set their own pace	Great deal of personal space, good decor, good tableware	High prestige
Mass	Low quality; little choice, poor presentation	Customers have the pace set for them	Small amount of personal space, poor decor, poor tableware	Low prestige

3

The Etiquette of Service:
The Expert Or The Friend?

Etiquette can be at the same time a means of approaching people and of staying clear of them.

(David Riesman, *The Lonely Crowd*, 1950)

Why People Eat Out

A restaurant is a stage where people play a variety of roles. Obviously it is a place where they come to eat and drink but it is also a place where they can meet and talk to one another. Of course some people come to try the food or because they are tired of cooking. Some, because they prefer to keep their relationships formal and specific, see the restaurant as a substitute for normal domestic entertaining. By dining 'out', they can meet and talk to others while preserving their own privacy. Others, however, want to put a space between themselves and those they know more intimately: the anonymity of the hotel or restaurant provides a welcome refuge from those with whom they share their personal trials, worries and everyday secrets.

There are also those who use the hotel as a second home. This kind of customer tries to build intimacy into the occupational relationship itself – to incorporate those who serve him as quasi-family members, by calling them by their first names, buying them drinks, giving them presents on their birthdays or at Christmas, and even on occasion leaving them money in his wills. What clues do these differences offer us? How far can they help us

50

to develop a body of rules which has wider application – which can contribute to a framework for a theory about hotel customers and their interaction with those whose job it is to serve them?

Anthropologists have long recognised that in all societies food and drink are used to mark social relations and to celebrate big and small occasions. But practically no work has been done, and certainly no general principles have been established, to develop this insight for comparative purposes. What we have in fact are two extremes. Starting with Lévi-Strauss (1970), we find meanings attached to food and drink that are universally applicable. And at the other extreme, there is ethnographic thoroughness but little systematic analysis (Mayer, 1960; Dumont, 1972). What is needed in this neglected area is a clearer understanding of the rules governing food and drink in a particular social system, from which to develop a method capable of more general application (see Douglas, 1972, pp. 61–80). This was the aim of a piece of research Nicod carried out with Douglas on British working-class families and the food they ate (Douglas and Nicod, 1974).

One feature they reported was that the dietary system possessed a cyclical pattern that was frequently and quickly repeated: families, for instance, tended to mark the week with a regular Sunday roast followed perhaps by hash on Mondays. They also found food preferences important as a basis for transactions within the family, and that individual likes and dislikes were the subject of constant negotiation. Thus the domestic menu itself was shown to be integrally linked to the social structure of the family; not only does it reflect that structure and the power relations between family members, but it also contributes to its form and provides the basis for transactions between the members. And when relations between family members break down, this too is reflected in their eating – as the experience of a family solicitor with whom we were discussing this material well illustrates. What constantly surprised him, when talking about marital breakdowns with his clients, was the number of instances he came across where the husband rejected his meal, and the relationship it signified, by feeding his food to the family pet.

51

By contrast, the menu in a restaurant, like those in magazines or cookery books, must be *independent* of local structuring and its pressures (although it will be oriented to the more standardised demands of the clientele). It is tempting to make a comparison between the domestic food system and what can be called the national food system to be found in restaurants and hotels. Such a comparison, though it cannot be taken too far, tells us about the importance of transactions that are associated with shared eating in both systems.

In a national system, the reason for variations in a menu can be fully explained not by reference to local social structuring, but by the food system itself and its budget. For example, the reason why a particular dish does not appear on a *table d'hôte* menu on a given day could be merely that it appeared on the day or at the meal before, or that a vital ingredient is too expensive.

On a domestic menu, however, the presence of a certain item will be the result of localised transactions. And the *form* that a meal takes is a reflection of the local social structure: for instance, whether it is chicken, leg of lamb, turkey, or a round of beef that appears before a family, if it is served at the high point of the week – Sunday dinner – the meat is invariably brought to the table in one piece, which symbolises the unity of the participants. It is also garnished with more than one vegetable and extra trimmings, and accompanied by a glass of beer or lemonade instead of plain water, all of which emphasise its place at the pinnacle of the domestic food week. This kind of eating and drinking is quite different from eating out in a restaurant, where theoretically it is possible to order 'Sunday dinner' every day of the week. In short, the restaurant menu lies outside the ordinary daily round of food-taking and it must not be confused with menus from the family food system.

But if we leave the food and the differences between the two menus, and concentrate on the negotiations and transactions that occur between the involved parties, we begin to understand their real significance. The main difference is that transactions taking place in a restaurant between those serving and those being served are altogether much more elaborate than anything likely to be found in the home. Indeed, they are so pronounced that they can serve as a marker in classifying different types of customer. There was a regular customer in our first high-level London hotel who was always served coffee in a large cup rather than the normal small one without his having to ask for it. And a couple in the Cardiff chain hotel who, whenever they came in for their Sunday lunch, always expected to find a bottle of wine waiting for them in an ice-bucket, with a wine waiter, corkscrew in hand, hovering ready to open it. One regular customer in our second high-level London hotel always expected to find his bottle standing upside down in the ice-bucket – all part of the 'silent language' of dining out! (See Hall, 1959.)

Many more examples could be cited to illustrate the point that food and drink transactions in restaurants are elaborate and varied, that they are a vital dimension of service and that, though service is individually negotiable, it operates within limits that are socially determined.

Open and Closed Transactions

Early in our research we became aware of the importance of the social role of shared eating and its effect upon relationships, both among customers and between customers and waiters. At first it was thought useful to create a typology of customers, based on the different terms waiters themselves use, in the same way Spradley and Mann (1975) had done in their study of an American college bar. We tried to arrange all the terms into a single folk taxonomy, much as an anthropologist might do for a set of kinship terms. This procedure led to a long list of terms, including the following:

resident	bastard
chance	bitch
regular	pig
perm	Mr Smith
person off the street	nice man

banquet	punter
party	prostitute
couple	stiff
businessman	peasant
management	snob
VIP	

It then became clear that waiters operate with several different *sets* of categories: some refer to the customer's length of stay ('resident', 'perm' or 'chance'); others indicate the size of a group ('banquet', 'party' or 'couple'). Still others can only be understood in terms of the specific context in which they are used: for example, a 'VIP' may be a person who has an important position in public life, the host to a banquet or large party, a person staying in the best suite, someone known to be a good punter, or even a particularly awkward customer. All customers are known as 'punters' – presumably an inverted comment on the waiter gambling on their tipping potential. Then there are some terms which have a regional character: for instance, in parts of northern England and in Scotland 'good for a drop' refers to a regular customer who is known as a good tipper. Awkward customers are variously described as 'bastard', 'bitch', and so on. 'Prostitute' is a term applied to women whose appearance suggests that they have been hired from an escort agency. 'Peasants' are people whose conduct and appearance give the impression that they are not accustomed to dining out. A 'snob' is someone who knows (or *thinks* he knows) how to behave and tries to draw attention to the fact whenever he can. A 'pig' is simply a person who *eats* a lot. And anyone who leaves without tipping is said to have 'stiffed' the waiter.

Important though it is for waiters to make such distinctions between types of customer, we soon found ourselves having to abandon this approach because its necessary discriminations were too subtle, its rules were too cumbersome, it was too unpredictable and dependent on unreliable verbal and appearance clues. Certainly, waiters often learn names and identities, classify people in terms of these specific social categories and perform their own role accordingly. But this was not sufficient to understand the complexities of the waiters' relationships with their customers. Indeed, it is unnecessary for waiters to know these classifications, even though they may have literally dozens of criteria for organising people into different categories.

What every waiter certainly must know, from the beginning of their first encounter, is into which kind of *transaction* the customer prefers to enter. 'Transaction', in this case, means anything which typically constitutes the common ground for social interaction. More specifically, it is related to the characteristics which define two distinct types of exchange between waiter and customer – hereafter referred to as *boundary-open* and *boundary-closed*. The boundary-open transaction includes the waiter in the relationships at the table; the boundary-closed kind essentially excludes him.

BOUNDARY-OPEN TRANSACTIONS

As the term implies, this type of transaction is not exclusive and can include a relatively wide circle of people within its scope. There is little emphasis on internal divisions, and relationships can encompass the host's family, close friends, business associates, distant relatives, or any mixture of acquaintances. Most important, it also includes the waiter himself.

In prestigious hotels, those entering into transactions of this kind tend to be customers who use the hotel as a second home. It was well known, for instance, that the poet and gardener Vita Sackville-West always used to be 'at home' at the Dorchester on the first Thursday of every month, and people who wished to see her could always find her there at that time – if, of course, they were prepared to pay for themselves (Nicolson, 1970). A businessman Nicod served at his highest-level London hotel told him: 'Rather than keep a flat in London, I always try to stay here on my way through Europe from Brazil.' One customer of the same hotel, who had been resident there for over twenty-five years, died at the age of ninety-seven and left £2,000 each to the two brothers, now first and second head waiters, who had served her faithfully over that period.

It is this kind of user who tends to foster intimacy, to incorporate waiters as quasi-family members and ask them questions about their own families. They are likely to offer reciprocal hospitality, 'If you should ever find yourself in Argentina . . . ', as well as to leave them money in their wills. Staff often develop strong feelings of attachment towards them too and, may well regard their death as a personal loss.

Oddly enough, we found the same kind of transactions taking place in the lower-level hotels. Here, however, it is not simply the surrogate-home customer, but almost all hotel guests who try to build intimacy into the service relationship and to incorporate the waiter within their social circle. This might involve some form of physical contact. One customer in Nicod's first northern hotel, for instance, asked if he would pose for a photograph with his hand on his wife's shoulder, 'Just so we'll be able to show the folk back home what a wonderful time we've had.'

Joking relationships of the kind observed in many societies around the world (Radcliffe-Brown, 1965: Bradney, 1957) also frequently develop here between waiters and customers. An American tourist staying at the same hotel asked Nicod whether he would like the autograph of a famous American athlete; when the dishes were cleared from the table the signature was discovered, written in black ink, and in letters an inch high, on the tablecloth. In addition, the waiter may become more closely involved through the diner's use of familiar language ('*Mum* will have the plaice, please'), as a result of asking the waiter's advice ('What wine would *you* recommend?') or sharing a joke or piece of personal news ('We'll have champagne; Harry's passed his exams').

BOUNDARY-CLOSED TRANSACTIONS

By contrast, boundary-closed transactions put a frame around the participants, who are more concerned with exclusion. Business diners, for the most part, prefer boundary-closed transactions and they use the hotel meal to develop intimacy between host and guest within the boundary. At the same time, such a host will 'freeze' and formalise relationships across the boundary. These excluding strategies both impress the guest and reduce the waiter to obvious subordination. It is as if the emphasis on ranking and protocol that occurs across the boundary encourages and enhances an equality and a common fellowship among those within it.

In this kind of transaction, hosts appear eager to stand on ceremony. They prefer behaviour that follows a format within a waiter/customer relationship that does not intrude. This kind of formality applies to both sides of the boundary. So long as the line between a host and his guest matters, then boundary closure between waiters and customers will be maintained by an emphasis on ritualised formality.

Nowhere is this more pronounced than in the multiplicity of 'rules' and the protocol which surrounds the serving of drink, affecting everything to do with the way it is poured, the temperature at which it must be stored, the length of time it has to be aired, the order in which it is served to guests, and the food that it 'goes' with. The host's sampling of a wine before it is served highlights the point – and is shown *in extremis* where the host insists on sampling a carafe or a bottle of cheap wine as if it were a more expensive one.

Boundary-closed transactions make the waiter particularly vulnerable to criticism and complaints, especially about failures to observe social etiquette or service 'protocol'. One customer complained about being given an ordinary knife and not a fish knife when he ordered plaice and chips in one of our low-level hotels. On one occasion Nicod was rebuked by a customer for serving him first, and not the woman whom he had not noticed sitting at the other end of the table: 'Have you no manners, Man?'

Protocol and Social Etiquette

Of course, in classifying transactions as boundary-open or boundary-closed, it should not be overlooked that a number of standard procedures in the service encounter must always be observed by both the waiter and the customer, and these do not vary. These include the rules for initiating an encounter and bringing it to an end; standard forms of response to particular words and actions; the rules for taking and terminating a turn at being served; and the obligation to refrain from certain activities in the presence of others.

It is useful to include some of these basic rules:

1   *Always serve a guest before you serve the host.* This rule takes precedence over everything else, and should always be observed whether it runs counter to other rules or not.
2   *Always serve a woman before you serve a man.* The problem, of course, is that nowadays a woman is very often the host, in which case she must be served last.
3   *Always serve an older person before you serve a younger one.* Here, again, older people acting as the host must be served last, and the woman accompanying an older man should be served first (but not if she is the host).
4   *Always address a customer by his or her surname, or as 'sir' or 'madam'.* Obviously, these forms of address demonstrate the deference of those serving towards those being served. In addition, the waiter should try not to put customers in a compromising position. Whether or not the people he is serving appear to be married, he should avoid the terms 'husband' and 'wife' in case they are not.
5   *Always serve from the left but clear dirty dishes from the right.* Although apparently not a matter of great importance, it is necessary that there is such a convention if waiters are to avoid colliding with one another. It is particularly important, say, for waiters at a crowded banquet, holding large service trays in one hand and serving with the other, to have some formal understanding so that they are better able to manoeuvre.

It might be assumed that a customer can very easily enter the kind of transaction he wants by instructing the waiter to modify certain general rules of this kind. Theoretically, this might be true if the purpose of these rules was simply to maintain front or put on a good show. In fact, the need to create a good impression is not so important as the need to maintain certain minimum standards. Obviously a diner can, and often does, tell the waiter that he does not mind being served out of sequence or from the right because he believes that this may help to build intimacy into the service relationship. But in this kind of situation boundary closure is not likely to be affected because these are rules which have been made *not* to be broken. Each of these rules has a specific function, and anyone who actively seeks, or at least condones, deviation from or non-compliance with them will be seen as trying to undermine the whole system.

To summarise, in both kinds of transaction formal understandings appear central, comprising what might be termed a dining etiquette which must always be obeyed. In terms of collision contingencies, such rules are to hotel staff rather as the highway code is to motorists. Sanctions will not necessarily be used against those who fail to comply with the rules, but there is always a risk that they may be brought to justice or penalised in some way.

Cues and Signals

In everyday life it is generally true that a person provides a reading of himself when in the presence of others. If unacquainted with him, others can glean clues from his conduct or appearance about what he will expect from them, what they may expect from him, and how best they should act to avoid conflict or to maintain goodwill. So, too, the waiter must learn the meanings attached to the cues or signals which people transmit so that he can distinguish the different types of diner and develop an appropriate set of responses. Learning how to classify and deal with the unknown diner by interpreting cues and signals has to be learned over time. With experience, the waiter can distin-

guish various types of customers according to the kinds of transaction that they would probably involve him in.

The way the diner and his companions are classified involves two
distinctly different kinds of sign activity. The first is the impression a person conveys of himself that is more or less sustained by
him, whatever he happens to be doing: an impression not specific
to the social setting in which he finds himself and that remains
constant over appreciable periods of time. Gender, age, race, class,
state of health will all be conveyed, in the main unwittingly, as the
part of a customer's make-up that can be thought of as the *primary
traits* of a diner's appearance.

Such fixed forms of display, because they are visual and easy to
discern, usually provide the waiter with sufficient evidence to
enable him to categorise his customers. The problem, however, is
that some customers or their guests may fall outside ready
classification: they may lack well defined primary traits or possess
traits which belong to different categories. Foreigners for instance,
are more difficult to classify than home nationals; their class rating
is often ambiguous and their expectations difficult to define,
particularly if they speak little English.

Secondly, then, in cases where people are not very easy to
classify, many crucial facts about the customer's identity can only
be elicited by closer inspection or through more direct communication than that required for the purposes of identifying primary
traits. For example, the diner's manner of dress, speech, gesture,
posture and bodily movements may enable a more accurate reading
to be taken. These forms of display are by nature a response to
something specific and relatively flexible. While it may be sustained at least for the duration of the social occasion, more often
the sign – say, a word or a gesture – conveys an immediate reaction
about events that are rapidly changing. These we shall call the
secondary traits of a diner's appearance, and by this we do not simply
mean the self-conscious gesticulation or 'body gloss' to which
Goffman has referred (1971, pp. 31, 154–71), but also those less
transient forms of expression which an individual can easily alter,
such as clothes, jewellery, cosmetics, and the like.

The Etiquette of Service: The Expert Or The Friend?

There is a wealth of folklore in the industry about eccentrics who have none of the defining traits – either primary or secondary – that is appropriate to their particularly high status. Stories are told of well-known lords, politicians and actors who appear in restaurants ragged, dirty, drunk or using crude language. These, which are impossible to authenticate, point up the anxiety that waiters experience in making their assessments on relatively little evidence. So far we have suggested that the customer possesses certain characteristics and that the standard reading that can derive from them will prove useful for a waiter in his dealings with the unknown diner. We have also suggested that the waiter acquires the ability to interpret these cues and signals over time. To elucidate the significance that his reading might produce, we now concentrate on his interpretation of the customer's primary traits: in particular, on the relationship which exists between the primary traits of the customer and those of the waiter serving him. In such matters as age, sex, place of origin and dialect, it appears that general rules apply to maintain congruency between the server and those served:

1   When a waiter and a diner are approximately of the same age, their transactions will tend to be boundary-open and not boundary-closed; whereas if they are not, the converse is true.
2   When a waiter and a diner come from the same country or place of origin, their transactions will again tend to be boundary-open and not boundary-closed; whereas if they do not, the converse is true. The same principle applies at a regional level – especially in respect of language which can create a social barrier, for instance, if one person has a strong regional dialect and the other speaks with an educated middle-class accent.
3   By contrast, when a waiter and a diner are *not* of the same sex, their transactions will tend to be boundary-open and not boundary-closed; whereas, if they are, the converse holds.

A male customer is more likely to build intimacy into the service relationship if a waitress serves him rather than a waiter. There is an assumption by men that waitresses should be more boundary open than waiters and they normally conform to this expectation. A single man, for instance, may want to set the stage for further interaction, and many waitresses do in fact get taken out by male customers. In highly prestigious hotels, however, behaviour related to sex-role differences does not take on the same significance, since no women are employed.

As suggested earlier, though, the accuracy of information provided by the primary traits depends a great deal upon customers being what they signify they are. Difficulties arise if the customer who enters a restaurant for the first time does not exactly fit any of the known stereotypes waiters use for purposes of classification. Thus gay couples dining outside their normal haunts can cause dissonance through their manner of dress, speech and behaviour. On one occasion a couple caused considerable consternation when one of them was suspected of being a transvestite. Similarly, if events occur during the interaction which contradict, discredit, or otherwise throw doubt upon the initial interpretation of the cues or signals that customers transmit, then the interaction may come to a confused and embarrassed halt.

Customers often oscillate between the two boundary-type extremes; for instance, in relation to the different types of company they keep. A man entertaining a group of businessmen will not usually drop his front before those who serve him, but when it comes to taking his wife out for dinner he may feel that he can be more open in his dealings with the waiter. Normally, the first time any middle-aged couple dine together in a particular restaurant, they would be expected to build intimacy into their relationship with the waiter. But for the couple discussing business over dinner, the very opposite may be true. To reduce the distance dividing those who serve from those served is to destroy the impression that most business people particularly seek to foster.

The waiter's main source of defining cues is the host rather than other guests at the table. But ambiguity can arise over who *is* the host, especially when – as is increasingly the case – women are hosting men in business negotiations. Such ambiguity is further increased when women who act as hosts offer men drink – traditionally, a male prerogative since it is a dangerous product, affecting consciousness as it does and being a common prelude to seduction. Such incongruity is most pronounced when a young woman as host, offers drinks to an older man. Many waiters cannot accommodate such role reversal and the dissonance it creates for them. In these situations they often attempt to manipulate the service so that it is the male guest who handles the drinks.

Where ambiguity surrounds the classification of customers, the waiter will generally try to find the conclusive proof he seeks in their secondary traits. Of these, the most important is the form of dress which people wear. Dress helps to define a customer's position because in most restaurants he has a wide range of choice in deciding what to wear. His freedom of choice distinguishes him from those who serve and provides great scope for individual expression. For men, the full range extends from jeans plus an open-necked shirt to a three-piece suit or even a dinner jacket, white shirt and black tie. For women it extends from jeans to a full-length evening dress. Somewhere within this range it should be possible to draw a line between those situations that express formality and those that are clearly informal. Admittedly this can only offer a rough-and-ready guide, but at least it helps to place people on the social map, enabling the waiter to clarify the nature and purpose of the diner.

Unfortunately the interpretation which can be put on dress in extremely prestigious hotels is not clear cut. Here, by tradition, there is a rule about wearing a jacket or a tie that applies to all men at dinner – although apparently not at lunch. In the evening, any man will be offered the loan of a tie, if it is simply this that is absent, or be denied entry if he has no jacket. The only exception to this rule is the man who is wearing ethnic dress of some kind, but the diner generally has no choice but to wear the prescribed clothing, no matter who he is, or what company he keeps.

The action taken by a restaurant manager against a customer

63

who is not wearing a jacket or tie when he enters a top-class establishment is a subject for endless anecdote. On one occasion, for instance, Elizabeth Taylor's son was turned away from our highest-level London hotel for wearing jeans and an open-necked shirt; much to the delight of the general manager, who thought the publicity would bring extra business. The incident was widely reported in the national press the next day.

Another way of getting customers who are not properly dressed to toe the line is to make them feel uncomfortable in the presence of others. For example, when a waiter in our first high-level London hotel noticed that there were two men without jackets or ties sitting at one of his tables, he turned to the commis who stood next to him and said: 'Well, really, I don't know where these people think they are!' This was said in such a way that those who were causing the offence could not fail to hear – and not long afterwards they left of their own accord.

Of all the cases Nicod came across personally, the most extreme was one which concerned a regular customer who arrived for dinner in Hotel 4 dressed in a polo-necked pullover. He explained that he had just arrived after a long day's drive and had not had time to go home and change. As the second head waiter who was telling the story put it: 'The best idea seemed to be for him to borrow someone else's clothes . . . fortunately we were about the same build and height and the shirt that I'd worn to work that day had just been washed and ironed. He was very grateful and gave me a fiver for helping him out.'

In cases where a clear understanding about who a diner is still does not emerge, the ambiguity that remains is seen as a potential threat by those who serve because the situation appears to have no predictable outcome (see Douglas, 1966). So rather than permit a customer to remain unclassified, the skilled waiter has to try to steer him to a position where he has a less ambiguous status – preferably, from the waiter's viewpoint as we shall see, into one of the two boundary-type extremes.

4

The Politics of Service:
'Who Gets the Jump?'

In this game, you've always got to be one step ahead. If you let the customer get the upper hand, before you know where you are he'll be treading all over you – and then it'll be too late to do anything about it. (Waiter, Hotel 5)

It might be assumed that a waiter cannot easily choose what line of treatment he receives from those he serves. Certainly it might be thought difficult for a waiter to influence the customers when he is so obviously of lower status than they are. But waiters can seize and hold the initiative by skilful manipulation and by using subtle aggression. This is what Whyte referred to in his Chicago restaurant study, as 'getting the jump on the customer':

> The first question to ask when we look at the customer relationship is: 'does the waitress get the jump on the customer, or does the customer get the jump on the waitress?' The skilled waitress tackles the customer with confidence and without hesitation. The relationship is handled politely but firmly, and there is never any question as to who is in charge.*

Clearly it is in the waiter's interest to control the service encounter, though being obviously 'in charge' is not necessarily the best tactic in the highest-level hotels. Nonetheless, if he handles his enounters skilfully, at worst, a waiter will be able to

*Whyte, 1946, pp. 132–3. This has been examined more recently in an empirical study by Butler and Snizek (1976), whose controlled experiments showed how the writer's skills in selling can increase the total bill and hence tips; see also Cooper and Oddie (1972).

forestall complaints rather than have to defuse them. And, at best, the customer can be given an impression that his every need and wish has been met, that he has been served with the correct blend of expertise and deference – in short, that he has had his money's worth and has every reason, therefore, to be generous with the tip. How then does the waiter set about manipulating his customers?

The first in any series of encounters is always the most crucial (Goffman, 1959a, pp. 22–3). For a servant in a service occupation this is particularly so. But for a waiter to take the initiative in a first encounter is especially difficult since the customer's attitude may have been set before the encounter by factors over which the waiter has no control. How a customer has been welcomed into the restaurant, where he has been seated, the atmosphere and decor – even events which took place before he came through the door, may all predispose him to a disagreeable non-compliance. The waiter may thus meet aggression of which he is not the cause. It will be his ability to deflect this away from himself, as well as by correctly interpreting the cues and signals he picks up from the customer, that will determine who really does 'get the jump'.

In this battle for who gets the jump, the control of space is vital: for the waiter it is crucial in affecting his earnings, his power and his prestige; for the customer it can make the difference between an enjoyable meal with good service or a spoilt meal soured by inadequate service.

Spacing and Placing

Although the significance of spatial cues often lies outside our consciousness, people of all cultures stake claims on space and attach meanings to them. Claims vary, of course, according to setting and the relative power of those involved. In the home, for instance, territorial rights include access to beds and privacy: who gets the best seating spaces near to or far from the window, the door, the kitchen, the television; who requires a quiet area in which to work. In large organisations, territorial rights are

66

fundamental to understanding different people's functions and powers: who is given an office of his own; who gets a key to the executive loo. Wherever people live, work or play, space must be divided up and allocated. In the home this may be done through indirect bargaining and direct appeals to physical needs (for example, 'babies need sleep' or 'the bread-winner needs rest'). But at work this is more likely to be in deference to office, to the exercise of authority, or out of respect for attributes such as age, skills, experience, length of service and dependability.

There are two sorts of territorial claims. The first we shall call a 'fixed' claim. It is staked out and attached to one claimant with permanent tenure. The claim exists for as long as the claimant holds the title deed or a particular office, and it cannot be acquired except through a direct transfer from the incumbent. Obvious examples are houses, fields, cars. Yet fixed claims can also apply to whatever area within a territory is clearly demarcated as belonging to one individual and not to another. The tables which are assigned to a waiter in a restaurant can be placed in this category.

The second type of territorial claim is a 'situational' claim. This is part of the permanent equipment in a fixed territory, yet is capable of providing temporary tenancy in sequence for a large number of different claimants. Unlike a fixed claim, it exists only as long as the claimant remains in possession. Park benches and hotel rooms are good examples (see Goffman, 1971, pp. 50–6), and so are tables in dining rooms and restaurants.

This distinction is, of course, only valid in degrees. A hotel room offers a situational claim, yet can function much like a house or other fixed territory, especially for those who regard the hotel as a second home. On the other hand, it can be argued that the only person with a fixed claim to restaurant tables is the proprietor, with the restaurant manager, the waiter and the customer all having nothing more than situational claims, albeit with varying degrees of permanency. But here it is useful to take only the customer's claim as situational, and the restaurant manager's and the waiters' claims as fixed.

Since people seldom isolate spatial cues but largely take them for granted, the hidden dimension of space comes to light only through close observation of its use. If we look at the tables in a restaurant, it might seem that they are distributed among waiters at random. In fact distribution of tables is far from haphazard; they are allocated according to informal ranking. Of paramount importance is the fact that the set of tables (called a station) which is ranked the highest should be the one most highly valued by customers, especially those known, or thought likely, to tip well. All other stations will then be graded accordingly because the system of ranking revolves around money – this being an essential part of the waiter's total rewards.

Where a waiter is permitted to keep his own tips, which station he is allocated will have a direct influence in increasing or decreasing his earnings. The manager therefore creates a greater obligation of personal loyalty towards himself in varying degrees by handing out the more lucrative stations on an individual basis. In other hotels, particularly the more prestigious ones, where tips are first pooled and then redistributed on a points system, preferential treatment involves a strong element of bureaucratic control, with those who serve the most important stations being awarded the highest number of points. In either case, the station allocation provides external proof of the waiter's status: the higher ranked the station, the higher are the rewards because his points will be higher.

At the same time because the higher ranked stations are assigned to core workers, this means that those served by them receive the highest possible standard of service. This is important because there is a particular type of diner – the regular customer, the resident of the most expensive suite, a person giving a large banquet – who would normally expect such a level of service. By being given one of the best tables, he will also automatically have one of the best waiters; the overall result is a mutually beneficial arrangement between those serving and those served.

Although spatial arrangement is largely determined by the physical layout of each restaurant, in the five hotels studied the way space is organised was basically similar. Therefore, in

68

analysing spatial arrangement, we start with assumptions about the nature of space which are widely held in all hotels. First, a premium is placed on privacy. Everywhere, space is both a matter of comfort and part of the physical background against which particular and immediate activities can take place. In a public place, because the opportunity for engaging others in undisturbed interaction is limited, privacy has special value. The restaurant tables normally most valued, therefore, are those near to or against the rear wall, well beyond the range of other people's voices or earshot, away from the noise of any band playing, and as far as possible from the sight and sound of the plate-wash or kitchen.

Other considerations, of course, are the decor and levels of personal comfort. Again, a scarce resource will often be involved, such as a table with comfortable chairs, one with a view or within easy reach of the dance-floor, a table with greater space between seats, or one which is decorated with flowers. Also included is the particular table over which a regular customer will lay claim because he feels 'more at home' at a table he can call his own. The same phenomenon is found in gentlemen's clubs, mental hospitals, old people's homes and domestic living rooms: claims tend to grow up around chairs and other property so that, although apparently available to anyone on a first-come basis, they take on the character of a fixed-territory claim by one individual, whether or not he is present. Obviously, many different individuals may have the same claim on a restaurant table. But because of relatively infrequent use, the same table can sustain different claims (see Woodbury, 1958; Lipman, 1967).

Finally, those who have tables near the restaurant's entrance tend to receive the manager's personal attention. Because the restaurant manager has the task of greeting customers upon arrival, his range of mobility is limited, for the most part, to an area immediately adjoining the entrance and to those tables in its close proximity. Therefore, those served within this zone receive better service, not least because the waiter himself is apt to do his best for them – knowing that his work is under the management's close scrutiny.

GREETING AND SEATING THE CUSTOMER

Once a customer enters the area where his presence functions as a summons, the restaurant manager or head waiter will normally provide a greeting and conduct him to an appropriate seat. If he is a regular or long-stay resident, he will be taken to his usual place – more often than not one of the 'best' tables, because he knows the layout and is allowed to choose where he sits. But if he is a 'chance' customer (that is someone off the street) or a short-stay resident, usually he must sit wherever the restaurant manager guides him. Sometimes even a regular may be obliged to sit where he is told or to share a table in a crowded setting. The sharing of tables does not occur, however, at the highest prestige levels. There are some cases, too, where an unknown diner may state his preference for a particular table and be permitted the use of it. Indeed, as we shall see, this is a good example of how a customer may seize the initiative, take control of the situation, and gain an advantage over the waiter.

Allocating an unknown diner to a particular table often involves complex criteria: not all of these apply in a given case, but some are more important than others. Among diners who are not well known, the most important principle in table allocation is simply 'first come, first served'. This unambiguously establishes the claim of an early arrival to be served at a better table than the person who enters later. This rule, however, can be varied by contingency: a party at the back of a queue often goes ahead when the appropriate number of places become available. Other factors include the customer's own preference if stated, and an assessment of his tipping potential.

Until events develop which provide the restaurant manager or head waiter with the conclusive evidence he needs to classify the customer, the latter's presence will take on a promissory character. Closely related to this need to classify customers is the fact that waiters do not agree on what are the best clues for predicting a customer's tipping potential. Nonetheless, when tables are allocated, assumptions are made about tipping and, since these are largely accurate, they confirm that a person's tipping potential can be assessed within broad limits. The 'tip', of course, has various possible meanings attached to it, but we shall follow Nailon's (1978) definition as: 'a gratuity voluntarily paid by customers directly to staff in an hotel or restaurant, over and above the price, whether a service charge is included or not, for the service provided'. (People do tip on top of the service charge, but less than 10 per cent: 5 per cent would be generous, 2 per cent acceptable.) In assessing tipping potential, the restaurant manager makes some major assumptions that inevitably influence the level of service that people receive:

1 *On average, men are considered better tippers than women.* The male customer is assumed to have greater experience of dining out and paying, and therefore knows the basic ground rules of the service relationship, especially what is an appropriate tip. This is why women on their own so often receive worse service than men.

2 *On average, a man accompanied by a woman is considered a better tipper than two men together.* A man feels under a greater obligation to display generosity and financial power when his guest is a woman.

3 *On average, the older person is considered a better tipper than the younger.* The older customer is more likely to know, through experience, what is the appropriate amount to tip. In addition, he can generally afford to tip more because he has more money.

4 *On average, customers with children are considered poor tippers.* People rarely tip in accordance with the effort and time which serving children involves. And people with children are thought to have less money than those without.

5 *People on package tours are considered to be low tippers.* These customers are often inexperienced, budget-conscious, and always ready to take advantage of cheaper rates; this only too often extends to reduced rates of tipping.

6 *Large parties are notorious for low tipping.* With smaller bills, the tip is proportionately high; but as the cost of the meal increases, a distinct fall-off occurs and those served in a large group rarely tip in the same proportion to the bills they receive as individuals (see Karen, 1962).

7 *The socially insecure are regarded as poor tippers.* People who are obviously nervous of eating out are regarded as too inexperienced and too poor to know about correct levels of tipping. In the same way foreigners are often regarded as essentially ignorant, especially in lower level hotels. The exception is a foreigner conforming to the stereotype of 'rich foreigner'.

PUTTING CUSTOMERS AT EASE

How comfortable customers will be in an unfamiliar setting, will depend, initially, on how the restaurant manager takes charge of the situation. When entering a restaurant for the first time, there can be little doubt that most customers have some feelings of uncertainty. Inexperienced diners may fear the threat of public exposure: improper attire and posture, inability to understand the menu, not using the cutlery correctly. But even one who is experienced and whose knowledge of the conventions gives him confidence, may be uncertain about the particular rules of the restaurant. Thus, it is safer for him to sit at any table the restaurant manager cares to give him. Only when he has patronised the establishment a few times will it be comfortable for him to demand a particular table (see Goffman, 1971, pp. 74–84; Lyman and Scott, 1967).

In his dealings with the customer, it is therefore imperative that the restaurant manager should relieve any anxieties and deep-seated suspicion that is felt in the preliminary stages. There are various methods of greeting diners, seating them at a table, handing menus to them, and taking orders that the restaurant manager can employ to put them at ease (for example, 'I've got just the table for you, sir'). But which particular form of greeting and seating is appropriate will depend upon what type of customer the restaurant manager is dealing with: whether he is the boundary-open or the boundary-closed type.

In the boundary-open case a joke or a light-hearted remark might help to put a customer at ease. The head waiter in our Cardiff hotel, upon showing customers to their table, would ask if

72

the woman would like a view of the sea, then point to a painting of the sea on the wall. Or, if a customer asked for steak, 'Well done!' he would say, 'I'll have it *cremated* immediately, sir.'

By contrast, when the situation is boundary-closed, it is better if the restaurant manager subordinates himself in the non-person role. To ease the customer's anxieties, he must visibly act within the prescribed limits of his official role, making sure that 'the customer is always right'. Consider the procedure of seating people at a table: first, the customers will be led to their table; then the restaurant manager will draw out the chairs and, with the flat of his hand, strike the top of them to get rid of any dust; then he will beckon the customers to sit down; and finally, once they are all seated, he will unfold their serviettes and place them on their laps. In fact, the first movement is the only one that can be said to be indispensable. Every succeeding move is not essential but helps to round out the performance. Some parts of the performance are, of course, omitted when those charged with the responsibility consider it unnecessary to observe the ritual. The point about the rules for opening and closing encounters is that protocol is strictly observed, and elaborated upon when the need arises. Boundary-openness brings a decline in ritual activity; boundary-closure supports it.

The Waiter Takes Over – But Who Takes Charge?

By the time the customer has his first contact with the waiter, he will have been influenced by the restaurant manager or the head waiter. Thus, the waiter must take over where the restaurant manager or head waiter has left off.

THE CUSTOMER TRIES TO GET THE JUMP

Tips
We examine the customer's position first because clearly he has an initial advantage over the waiter. His single most important

advantage comes from the practice of tipping. Undoubtedly there are some people who never tip – figures for those who never do vary considerably, from about 4 per cent (*Which?*, June 1968) to 88–92 per cent (NEDO, 1975b) – but it is this very element of uncertainty – 'will he or won't he' – that puts the customer a step ahead. This is especially so when the diner is unknown and his tipping potential cannot easily be assessed.

The prospect of a high tip may even provide the basis for outright bribery – for a suggested collusion between customer and waiter at the expense of the hotel (Mars, 1982: 149). Hotel folklore provides many variations on this theme. For instance, there is the customer who enters a restaurant for the first time, tears a £10 note into two, offers one half to the waiter and then promises to give him the second half if he is satisfied at the end of the meal. In the first hotel we studied, someone, on the first day of his stay and before being served his first meal, gave £5 to the restaurant manager, £5 to the chef and £5 to the waitress. It was clear that a further payment of the same kind might be expected at the end of his stay if he was pleased with the service. Nicod recalls people in the same hotel saying: 'Give us much of everything as you can, my lad, and we'll see that you're all right.'

An exchange of desirables therefore occurs but, because the relationship is not egalitarian, the balance is easily upset. Too much or too little can easily disturb it. Over-tipping, on the one hand, may have the effect of reinforcing the customer's position of socio-economic superiority. One customer in our first high-level London hotel gave Nicod a £2 tip for doing no more than serving him vegetables, a normal part of the commis' job. But there are instances when the opposite is true: customers often given an inadequate reward for the service they receive; sometimes they leave nothing at all. The extent to which this upsets those who serve indicates that non-monetary factors are involved. In describing how some customers will sit at a different table on their last day so they can avoid whoever has been serving them during their stay, a waitress in the first hotel we studied said: 'It's not that I really mind whether someone gives me a drop or not . . . it hurts, though, when someone is so mean that he won't even say "Thank you".'

Whyte (1969) quotes a waitress on the subject:

> You think of all the work you've done and how you've tried to please those people, and it hurts when they don't leave anything for you. You think, so that's what they really think of me . . . It's like an insult.

For many waiters or waitresses, the greatest insult, however, is to receive such a small tip that they feel degraded, embarrassed, nonplussed, or otherwise upset at having to accept it. Some thought that it was better to receive nothing at all than be given an amount which was totally unrepresentative of the service they provided. One waitress in Hotel 1 said that, if she had served a large family with children for one or two weeks, and then was given a 10p piece, she would give the money back, saying, 'It's all right, thank you, I've got enough change for my bus fare home.'

Others were glad of the service charge which meant they did not have to depend so much on what they earned from tips. A waiter in our first high-level London hotel had always been asked by a regular customer to fetch a box of matches for him:

> He used to give me a shilling and in the old days it seemed quite a lot . . . but now when he comes here and give me a 5p piece, he still expects me to be grateful. Well, I mean to say, we wouldn't last long if we had to rely on people like that.

What, then, emerges is a two-way exchange, one individual providing goods or services, the other providing a sign of appreciation. Like the universal gift, the tip received for service may normally be expected, but can never be demanded; it is meant to measure appreciation of a relationship, not the exchange value of work done. Something given – service – must typically be returned with something of equivalent value – a tip. And a tip need only be offered if the relationship calls for it, it cannot be pressed for as an economic right. It is quite different, therefore, from a commercial exchange where it is agreed in advance what is to be exchanged. With a tip, the emphasis is on the relationship between the customer and the waiter and the quality of this is manifest in the service offered and received.

Special Requests

Obviously the basic reward that waiters receive is economic payment, the money management pays for a basic level of service. However, the customer may also reward the waiter on a personal basis by tipping. The direct dependence on the customer for tips is more accurately construed, not as a reasonable mark of payment for basic service, but rather as a mark of appreciation for providing some *additional* service that might not normally be expected. So, too, customers may sometimes not only tip for a service the waiter renders of his own accord but for something they have asked him to do as a special favour. They thus make a claim for something they have no right to demand, but which they may expect in return for a tip.

One customer in our first high-level London hotel asked for a spring onion with his cheese. Although spring onions were out of season the waiter went to the kitchen to find what they had to offer and returned, saying, 'May I bring you a finely chopped Spanish onion instead, sir?' This was service above the expected normal and worthy of a tip. A similar example was provided by a customer in the same hotel who, whenever he came for lunch, always ordered a watercress and onion salad – something not on the menu, but which he received without even having to ask for it.

The customer who wants to be a step ahead may make a special request simply to enable him to take control. It is a kind of game in which the customer pits himself against the waiter's wits and can score points easily. Waiters often feel they have little choice but to accept most claims which customers exert. In some cases, the waiter may even anticipate what the customer wants and grant him a favour without being asked. Though this helps the waiter to retain some control, he is always vulnerable because the customer can so easily change his mind. On one occasion, for instance, the customer who always had the watercress and onion salad, rebuked a waiter for bringing it, saying 'I don't remember ordering *this*', as if he had never eaten it before in his life. So normally the waiter has little room for manoeuvre. He must simply accept his subordinate status as part of the 'primary adjustment' required of him. We therefore conclude that customers have a greater capacity to seize control and take advantage of the situation, especially in its initial stage.

Complaints

Tips and gratuities, and the degree of customer satisfaction these imply, provide a positive measure of how a waiter's performance is judged by his colleagues. Conversely, it is also possible to measure the waiter's performance in negative terms, by looking at the number and frequency of complaints he receives. In fact, this is the measure usually adopted by managements. If a waiter is to satisfy both his bosses *and* his customers, knowing how to defuse complaints before there are serious repercussions becomes a crucial skill, and therefore an important part of his professionalism.

In cases where a complaint is about food and it appears to have been made sincerely, the remedy is simple: the waiter returns the food to the kitchen and asks the chef either to alter or replace it. When the complaint is that the food is undercooked, for instance, it can usually be put back in the oven or under the grill. It is more difficult when the customer complains about the food being overcooked because the chef must be asked to prepare another dish. As this will involve additional costs, the waiter must assess how far the customer's complaint derives from ignorance of what he should actually expect, and how far it is really true. One customer in our first high-level London hotel complained about her steak being overcooked because it 'looked charred'. In fact she had ordered it 'well done', and it did not look particularly charred. Rather than give her another steak she would still dislike, the waiter invited her to choose something completely different.

There are cases where a complaint is not genuine, and the customer does not honestly believe in it either: the complaint is

77

simply a means of drawing attention to his own importance. One customer in our first hotel had a great reputation for complaints of this kind. Before she entered the restaurant she would complain in the women's toilets about the colour of the wallpaper. Once in the restaurant the butter would be too cold, the carafe of white wine too sweet, the meat too tough, and so on. Nothing can be done to satisfy this kind of complainant because no sooner has the original complaint been dealt with than new ones are invented. Indeed whether such customers' complaints are dealt with hardly matters.

Finally, there are complaints which are a blatant attempt to obtain a reduction in the cost of a meal, or even to obtain a free complimentary meal. The best example of this is the customer who sends a letter of complaint – a 'big con', in waiters' terms, because the customer is invariably thought to be 'trying it on' to get a complementary meal. Waiters resent having to serve someone who has done this. First, the mere fact that he appears to be 'getting something for nothing' does not seem right to them. Secondly, and more importantly, most people, if given the opportunity, order the best of everything but fail to show their appreciation at the end of the meal. Thus, as the wine waiter in our first London hotel put it:

> After a while, you get to know them. A fellow had a meal on the house the other night. He ordered the most expensive dishes, a top bottle of wine, two double brandies and, to cap it all, asked if he could have the framed photograph of the cabaret artist from off the wall. I wouldn't even mind so much if he'd shown his appreciation, but the mean bugger didn't leave a thing.

In cases where a complaint appears genuine, or at least where the customer honestly believes it to be so, the manager will generally take action against the waiter. In the first hotel we studied, for example, the manager decided he had no choice but to dismiss a waiter for swearing. The waiter had been about to serve some customers when he discovered that his tray and serving cloth were missing. 'Where's my fucking tray? What the hell've you done with my bloody cloth?' he shouted to someone at the other end of the dining room. Judging by the number of complaints, this had upset a large number of people and instant dismissal was automatic.

On the other hand the waiter may rely upon the manager's support to put the customer in his place when a customer's claim is unreasonable. In our first London hotel there was a general rule that no one should be served between eleven and twelve o'clock during the cabaret. Those who arrived shortly before 11pm were warned about this. One night a customer who arrived late claimed he should not have to pay the service charge because of the long delay in service during the cabaret. But when the waiter threatened to call the manager, the customer immediately paid the bill in full. Knowing he had no right to press the claim, he preferred to maintain front by withdrawing it before it was too late to do so.

Some complaints are not so easy to define and the stance adopted by the manager may be ambivalent. Here we refer to the kind of claim which may not be authentic and yet must be taken seriously – at least until it is known to be invalid, exaggerated, or based on a false premise. In this kind of situation, the manager may often give the waiter a public dressing-down for the complainant's benefit, but in fact his relations with staff are left unimpaired or even strengthened by backstage activity designed to contradict this impression and build up lines of defence against the customer. A waiter in our first London hotel was called to a customer's table at the end of his meal and told to wait while a long list of complaints was written on the serviette. These included slow service, food undercooked, food overcooked, cold food, and so on. Then the customer insisted that the waiter should show this list to the manager. The manager's immediate reaction was to come over and apologise personally, but once behind the scenes he made it clear to the waiter what he really thought of the customer: 'What a bastard, he doesn't even have the courtesy to write on a piece of paper'.

THE WAITER TRIES TO GET THE JUMP

Although the customer is more likely to have the advantage over the waiter than vice versa, we find that the waiter, however passive his

79

role may appear, will himself have some control. Usually both parties in a service encounter are sufficiently attuned to each other's role to avoid open confusion. The maintenance of this surface of agreement, this veneer of harmony or working consensus depends on each party feeling obliged to pay lip service to a crude overall definition of the situation. But people define situations in different ways. Thus, between waiter and customer in boundary-open transactions, a reciprocal show of affection, cordiality and good-will towards the other is maintained. In a boundary-closed trans-action, on the other hand, the waiter takes on the role of service specialist, anxious not to become too involved with the personal problems of his client, while the customer responds, from a standpoint of social distance, with a show of respect for the competence and integrity of the waiter performing his role.

Boundary-breaking Devices

When there is a clear understanding that those being served share some, but not all, of the defining features of a boundary-open transaction, the waiter's ability to seize the initiative will often depend upon whether he can break down the remnants of the boundary dividing the server from the served. One waitress, when serving a family with a young child, for instance, would often adopt the following strategy. As soon as the family were seated and waiting to give their order, she would approach their table and then deliberately knock over the child's drink. In doing this, she would make it appear to be the child's fault. She would then take the initiative in sorting out the mêlée this caused, and at the same time put the whole family under an obligation to her. 'Don't worry, he's only a baby – I can easily get him another.' It is difficult for those of higher status to maintain formality and social distance when there is such an imbalance of obligation owed by them to those of lower status. This strategy had a further advantage for the waitress because she could arrange this switch in initiative without causing any loss of face on her customers' part, since it is generally agreed that children are irresponsible, not fully socialised and apt to cause accidents.

80

There are other devices involving the waiter performing minor acts of kindness and thereby ingratiating himself with those served. Often 'non-person' categories are selected for such treatment: for example, the very young, the very old and the physically handicapped. The waiter helps the old or the infirm, fetches high-chairs for children too small to sit at table, offers free advice about what food is appropriate, even passing remarks about their appearance or conduct. Physical contact is common to ingratiation. A waitress in our second northern hotel, when serving a family with children, for example, always used to run her fingers through the youngest child's hair, saying: 'What wonderful curls you've got. If only I had lovely hair like yours.' Given that there is uncertainty as to what kind of intimacies are permissible, it is safer to first build familiarity into the relationship with those who are not full participants. The possibility of more familiar forms of communication with this type of customer then paves the way for breaking down the barriers more generally.

The printing of menus in French, a feature in nearly all higher level hotels, tends to shift the initiative to the waiter. His advantage arises because of uncertainty that its use causes a surprisingly high percentage of customers. One indeed cannot help but feel that this mystification is being deliberately fostered by many hotels as part of the English obsession with maintaining and enhancing social distance. Two American tourists complained in our second high-level London hotel because, after travelling for two months in Europe, they had looked forward to their arrival in England where people spoke their own language: 'But what do we find when we get here? . . . A menu written in French just like the rest of the Continent!'

When a waiter comes across customers who obviously stumble over the French terms for food, he has increased flexibility in shifting the transaction to either the boundary-open or the boundary-closed mode. He can, that is to say, adopt the role either of friendly adviser or of relatively distant service specialist.

Some strategies, particularly in lower prestige restaurants, are especially designed to deritualise the waiter's performance. For example, some waiters swear in public to good effect: 'Oh bugger, I've dropped the bloody peas.' (In this case, words which caused one waiter to lose his job, were used here to accelerate intimacy between those served and those who serve. Much depends on the way the words are used to convey a particular meaning.) Others use slang, colloquialisms, expletives and familiar forms of address; or perhaps crack jokes, grin, or make light-hearted remarks designed to reduce the possibility of boundary-closure. One waiter in our first northern hotel hit upon the novel idea of dispensing with a written menu at breakfast. Instead, he would recite it from memory. Then, if challenged, he would say 'You don't really need a menu . . . I'm a "walking menu" and I'm much better than the ordinary kind . . . I can tell you things you won't even find on the menu.'

Taken together, devices of this kind provide a basis for the co-operative activity that follows. They are not, of course, part of the organisation's official strategy, but the impression the waiter is giving typically is not inconsistent with it. However, other strategies, if not kept a secret from the customer, *would* contradict and discredit the impression officially being fostered. Customers can be treated respectfully, face-to-face, then ridiculed, gossiped about, caricatured, cursed and criticised when the waiters are backstage: here, too, plans may be worked out for 'selling' things, 'touting' for tips or employing 'angles' against them.

Touting for tips takes several forms. For example, the waiter can provide larger portions, extra items, coffee with cream instead of milk, or special items normally in short supply, such as melba toast, or petits fours. This is often preceded by a phrase such as 'Would you like any extra . . . , sir?' to make the customer aware that such treatment is provided as a special favour. It also means that the waiter may delay commitment or extricate himself from the situation, should the customer's response be inappropriate. One waitress in our second northern hotel asked a customer if he was 'a big breakfast eater'. His reply, 'I'm a big eater of every-thing', left her in no doubt where he stood. So, too, waiters often test the customer out with offers of extra ice cream, cheese and

biscuits, tea, coffee, or cake – all items not readily accounted for –
before they actually serve the goods. If the response is right, and
they know that there is some guarantee that the time and effort
they have invested will bring greater financial reward, they will
then take the risk.

Operating Outside the Boundary

In the final analysis, though, the waiter must always show a proper
concern for the trust placed in him by the people he serves: if a
customer demonstrates complete faith in the waiter's judgement,
nothing should be done that may destroy or damage this trust. For
instance, if a waiter is asked to recommend something on the
menu, he should suggest a wide range of dishes, not merely the
most expensive ones. And the price of what the customer orders
should make no difference to the service he receives. Similarly, the
wine waiter in our second high-level London hotel thought that it
was wrong to fill people's glasses to the brim. Quite apart from the
fact that the wine's bouquet could not be fully appreciated, it made
people drink faster and order more than they really wanted.

Whatever the waiter does, then, to ensure that he has control of
the situation, it must always lie within the accepted limits of the
service relationship. A waiter may advise, suggest, influence,
persuade, badger, or cajole – but he must never *appear* to dictate
from inside the boundary. Indeed, particularly in higher status
hotels, a waiter may find it easier to control transactions from
outside the boundary. Here the parties engaged in the transactions
maintain the spirit of those consummating a coldly bargained
agreement, not exchanging favours. Thus in such higher status
hotels – whose staff can be categorised as being 'craft-oriented' –
a waiter will take particular pride in the skills he uses to manipulate customers from the outside; and it is here that the service
specialist is supreme.

Nonetheless, in boundary-closed transactions, the subordinate
nature of personal service means that a waiter frequently feels a
resentment that must remain unarticulated. While not wishing to
render customer satisfaction impossible, a waiter may use his

service skills to cheat or insult the customer, or at least cause some indefinable disquiet. To do this he must use strategies that combine subtle aggression with what should be able to pass for good professional conduct (e.g. Fuller and Currie, 1966). One waiter we knew had developed a particularly effective method of inducing dissonence – especially when directed at the socially insecure. He would repeat all the orders offered by the customer in French but would do so with an emphasised accent at each repetition. He was able thereby to suggest that the hapless customer was obviously unused to expensive eating out because he could not even pronounce the names of the dishes correctly!

Before he can engage in this kind of aggression, a waiter must first establish visibly that he is acting within the prescribed limits of his official role and that, on the surface at least, he accepts certain moral obligations. Thus, some customers prefer him not to intrude or come too close because they can never be sure to whom he will convey their secrets. Knowing this, the waiter may lower his voice as he enters their presence, throwing himself, as it were, into the role of being seen but not heard. In doing so, he appeals to those he serves to treat him as if he were not present; as someone who can be relied on to keep their secrets and not betray their trust. In our high-level London hotels, the waiters frequently dropped their voices to a whisper whenever they entered a customer's presence.

Interestingly, eighteenth-century accounts suggest that it was the difficulty in keeping secrets from servants that led to the acceptance of the 'dumb waiter' – originally a tiered table stocked with food, drink and eating utensils, from which guests served themselves. Upon the introduction of the dumb waiter in England, Mary Hamilton (quoted in Hecht, 1956, p. 208) reported:

> My cousin Charles Cathcart din'd with us at Lady Stormont's: we had dumb-waiters so our conversation was not under any restraint by ye servants being in ye room.
>
> At dinner, we had ye comfortable dumb-waiters, so our conversation was not obliged to be disagreeably guarded by ye attendance of Servants.

84

A second distancing technique the waiter can employ is to make use of politely formal terms, such as 'sir', 'madam', 'Mr X', or 'Mrs X', whenever he addresses customers directly. Behind their backs he may refer to them by bare surname, first name, nickname, or some title which relegates them to an abstract category: for example, 'pig', 'peasant', 'snob', 'regular'. If the waiter wishes to maintain some dignity while making clear the disrespect he really feels, he may adopt a slighting pronunciation, say, an exaggerated emphasis upon the 'sir' or 'madam'. Given that customers are treated relatively well to their faces, they cannot isolate discourtesy implied by the tone of voice, mannerisms, innuendoes, or double entendres that the waiter may use to heap abuse or familiarity upon them. Nor can customers, by implication, effectively bring an official complaint against a waiter without more substantial evidence than merely subtle discourtesy.

We have suggested two standard ways in which waiters keep their distance – by lowering their voices and through politely formal terms of address. So long as the line is sustained, the waiter can then freely use his special knowledge and experience to derogate the customer's dignity with impunity. Because of the mass of rules and (often spurious) expertise surrounding dining out and social etiquette, as the specialist the waiter is ultimately always in a stronger position than those he serves. A good example of this occurred in our second London hotel when a customer complained that the brandy he had been given was not Rémy-Martin as he had ordered, but a less expensive one. By taking the glass back and returning impassively with it a little later, the waiter managed to create the impression that the brandy *might* have been changed for the kind which the customer had ordered. On the other hand it might not. In fact, it was the same glass of brandy and the customer had been deceived, but it would take a particularly confident customer to send it back a second time.

Similarly, a customer may lower his defences in the waiter's presence – making a special request or a 'faux pas', showing signs of nervousness or plain ignorance. Then the customer puts himself at the mercy of those serving him. This is embarrassing enough,

85

but if a special favour is refused, or if his nervous disposition, his ignorance, or his mistakes are openly admitted, he will suffer greater humiliation. Rather than risk getting into such a position, a waiter may opt to pass the whole thing off as a joke – thus getting the jump without quite acting outside the prescribed limit of his role. For instance, when a customer complained in our second London hotel because there were no English cigars on sale, the waiter replied, half jokingly and half seriously:

> I'm very sorry, sir, but I can't offer you English cigars . . . as you're probably aware, sir, we don't grow tobacco in this country. Perhaps you'd care to choose one of our very fine Havana cigars instead?

Perhaps the cruellest treatment that waiters can mete out is when a customer makes a complaint or orders something, and this is formally acknowledged, but then he receives something he did not really bargain for. Thus whenever someone ordered lobster bisque in our first London hotel, he was frequently taken by surprise to find the brandy poured into the soup and lit. Those who did not know better would wait several minutes until the flames subsided. Depending upon whether he wanted to 'give the customer a hard time', the waiter might intervene and show him how to dip his spoon into the soup and not get burnt. So, too, a wine waiter in the Cardiff conglomerate hotel always put on an excessive display for people who had ordered an expensive brandy. This was not to please but to patronise them. First, holding it by its stem, he would twist the brandy glass over a lamp, passing it in and out of the flame until it reached the right temperature. He would then pour a little brandy into the bottom and tilt the glass towards the lamp, allowing the liquid to catch fire and then turning the glass round in his hand until the flames went out. Finally, he would pour more brandy into the glass until it was about a third full – so that the bouquet could be fully appreciated, at which point he would deliver it with a flourish.

This waiter got the jump by an elaborate display of craft expertise. The same result may be achieved by reversing the strategy: by putting on an equally conspicuous display of incompetence, presented as a willingness to go to extremes, in order to meet customers' expectations which are inappropriate. One waitress explains:

> I remember one family coming in that looked right out of place, not frozen steak types, frozen faces, though. Son in his midtwenties, mother and sister, I should think. He had tiny little feet with very highly polished shoes. I couldn't help noticing because he didn't once look at me while he was ordering, kept swinging his foot up and down and watching that. They got on to the wine list, which had one or two reasonable ones – nothing special – and after a big discussion he asked me for a bottle of Mateus Rosé, 'well-chilled'. We kept a couple in the fridge door, so I brought one of those through. Wouldn't do at all: 'I said "chilled", not cooled.' I looked as sorry as I could, went back to the bar and got the big iron bucket we used for tipping the slops into. I filled it up with all the ice I could find – great big blocks – stuck the bottle on top and brought the whole lot back into the restaurant. I had to lift it over people's heads, so they all noticed. I put it on a spare table – they were small and very close together – and said, 'That should be chilled in about a quarter of an hour, sir. Would you like your starter now?' He tipped me about 20 per cent of the bill. (Waitress, Steak house)

The same informant provided us with a downmarket example of maintaining – or retrieving – dignity by conveying disrespect for the customer in such a way that it provides no clear ground for complaint.

> Sometimes a party of half-a-dozen would come in and you could tell before they'd even sat down that they'd want the cheapest meal we did. But they'd spend ages eating all the rolls, drinking water and pretending to discuss it. Then, 'Miss! We'd like to order now, please', and a hand pulling at your sleeve if you were hovering too close. I'd usually have the order written down already, or pretend to, so I could look straight at them while they went round the table: 'I *think* I'll have the plaice and French fries'; 'Yes, that'll do

me – I'm not very hungry'; 'Well, I won't be difficult.' Then I'd look at my pad and nod: 'Six fish and chips – right away, sir.'

Finally, if a customer chooses to put the waiter under pressure, he may be mistreated or 'taught a lesson' to his face. Where the waiter is abused by those he serves, he may well decide that the relationship has 'blown' and cannot be restored. In such circumstances he may aim to cause humiliation or discomfort – at least to the extent that a real transition takes place in relative power, standing and authority. When a customer complained loudly in our second London hotel that he had been brought a plate of scallops when he had ordered mussels, the waiter knew that he had made no mistake, but gave him the opportunity to choose again. The customer then asked for a lobster or prawn salad but did not specify which. The waiter, choosing to cause him the maximum possible inconvenience and expense, ordered the dressed lobster, the most expensive item on the menu, which took twenty to thirty minutes to prepare (the prawn salad at a third of the price would have taken five minutes). Customer complaints can usually be coped with: the aim is to contain them. When they are delivered loudly, and are therefore made public, however, containment ceases to be an option.

5

The Waiter's Formal Career: Learning To Be Straight

In the nature of things, you can hardly expect to start anywhere except at the bottom. First of all, your job will be to scrape food off the plates that come from the dining-room before they go to the scullery to be washed. You will receive forty francs a month for this employment — an almost exaggeratedly high salary, as your expression seems to indicate. Moreover, it's not customary when conversing with me to smile before I myself smile. I am the one who gives the signal to smile. *Bon.*

(Thomas Mann, *Confessions of Felix Krull, Confidence Man*, 1973, p. 178)

Every occupation has its own set of rules prescribing behaviour at a particular stage. Once the individual has demonstrated sufficient ability and willingness to learn, in the normal course of events he will then pass to the next stage, or 'status' (Van Gennep, 1960). Every stage will vary in terms of the skills, personal attributes and underlying values that are involved, and the length of time the individual will expect to spend in it before looking for promotion. In occupations where there is a strong element of bureaucratic control, standard procedures for advancement are common and passage through the various stages is strongly marked by a clearly defined office or status position. In less structured occupations the individual has more latitude for creating his own position or choosing from the existing ones, but he has less *certainty* of achieving any particular status. A comparison of the career of a civil servant with that of an actor illustrates this clearly.

89

In order to understand the type of career that is normally open to waiting staff in the hotel industry, we take Hughes' definition of 'career' (1958, p. 63):

> A career is the moving perspective in which the person sees his life as a whole and interprets the meaning of his various attributes, actions, and the things which happen to him. This perspective is not absolutely fixed either as to points of view, direction or destination . . . A study of careers . . . may be expected to reveal the nature and 'working constitution' of a society. Institutions are but the forms in which the collective actions of people go on. In the course of a career the person finds his place within these forms, carries on his active life with reference to other people, and interprets the meaning of the one life he has to live.

It follows that, since the range of 'institutions' loosely described as hotels is so broad, we would expect to find widely differing career patterns among waiters. Our research confirms this. At the *craft* end of the hotel spectrum, in top level hotels, the emphasis is on technical skill and professional expertise, and work roles are defined according to these criteria. In a high-prestige establishment, such as the Dorchester, the Savoy, or the Ritz, it is easy to create a pyramidal ranking system based on skills for which appropriate rewards can be offered. This pattern is also found in the large conglomerate-owned hotels which are highly *bureaucratic* and have modelled themselves – with a fair degree of success – on the high-prestige type. Characteristically these hotels have tried to formalise rewards and tighten up on fiddles.

The highly prestigious hotels, however, with their emphasis on craft skills, not only supply a model for the organisation of lower level hotels but they also supply the core of their senior staff. They act as training establishments and as such contain a large number of perpetually replaced peripheral workers who see their employment as providing experience they can exploit later on. Just as Sandhurst represents the Army training school par excellence and Oxford and Cambridge the apex of the university system and academic career structure, there are a small number of highly prestigious hotels which fulfil a similar function in providing seed-bed institutions and a training-ground for the hotel industry. When Nicod began work as a commis in hotel 4, he was told:

> This is no ordinary hotel . . . it's like a teaching hospital where people come to learn the trade . . . and you'd better try to forget anything you might have picked up . . . it's better if you start again at the very beginning. (Station head waiter, Hotel 4.)

Many people who work in the more prestigious hotels regard their limited stay as an apprenticeship that defers greater rewards until later. Indeed they are often low paid but they regard their immediate financial return as less important than the better training and experience which can only be had in such establishments. Their economic loss is something to be borne in the short term so they can obtain higher paid jobs later. As one Italian who had just left a better paid job to work in hotel 4 put it:

> I was getting more money at the last place . . . but then I don't really mind because I'm only working here for the reference . . . and when I go home it'll help me get a much better job. (Commis, Hotel 4.)

The passage through the ranks can be a long protracted process in a high-level hotel. Not so long ago a commis might work 10 years in the same establishment before he could expect promotion to the next rank. Even today, a waiter might work for 5 years as a commis until eventually he is offered a station head waiter's post.

At the other end of the spectrum, in the sector we term *entrepreneurial*, there are only relatively slight differences in status, and jobs have little formal or precise definition. Although a wider variety of skills must be mastered, the emphasis here is less on service *per se* and more on speed, the ability to cope in critical periods and on reliability. Staff are more concerned with the short term, and in it to maximise their own entrepreneurial opportunities; in other words, their returns from fiddles. This loose structuring, coupled with high informal rewards, is found usually lower down the hierarchical scale, in the small, traditional, independently run hotels that still dominate the industry, despite the growth of the conglomerate-owned sector.* A similar lack of stratification is characteristic of those middle-level *bureaucratic* hotels where the service ideal and the reality rarely, if ever, correspond. Here the constant effort to maintain front, in what we have called 'the ambiguous middle', requires a degree of flexibility and adaptability from staff which precludes the setting-up of a clearly defined status hierarchy. Access to informal rewards remains an important criterion in judging career success.

This chapter focuses on the conventional, stratified career of the craft waiter, where there is an upward progression through a series of well-defined stages – each clearly marked by a status label, a finite area of responsibility, a distinctive style of dress and a code of permitted behaviour. Access to informal rewards is commensurate with the individual's proximity to the core, and the position he has achieved in a hierarchy constructed on the basis of technical skill rather than a capacity for *ad hoc* inventiveness.

Rites of Passage

Typically, a craft recruit begins as a commis waiter and becomes, in sequence: a demi-chef; a chef de rang; a station head waiter; a first head waiter, and a restaurant manager. Obviously how the change in status is achieved – or as Strauss (1959, p. 92) puts it, 'How a person *becomes* something other than what he once was' – is of crucial importance. What must happen at the intermediate stage if status passage is to be effective is our particular concern.

The intermediate stage commonly has three essential characteristics. One is that beginners are normally expected to learn the rudiments of the waiter's craft on the job. In effect, this means that

*NEDO figures show that the industry is dominated by small primarily unlicensed establishments – and this despite the existence of the well-known giants of the industry. Out of the total of 33,700 hotel establishments, some 20,700 (over 61 per cent) have between 4 and 10 bedrooms – out of which some 14,000 are unlicensed and located mostly at the coast; see NEDO, 1976, pp. 8–18.

they are taken through a particular set of tasks by an experienced hand until they are judged sufficiently competent to work on their own. There is always a danger that novices may be attached to a worker who is ill-qualified to train them. But because their work involves direct contact with those they serve, the 'sitting next to Nellie' approach must always play an important part in the learning process (Boella, 1974, pp. 55–66). Moreover, the strategies waiters use for dealing with and manipulating customers are, in effect, professional or trade secrets. If the teacher-pupil relationship is strictly one-to-one, it is less likely that facts which are not public knowledge may 'leak' beyond hotel staff and the illusion of 'good' service thus be destroyed.

Secondly, dress is obviously a useful symbol of group membership and a marker of status within that group. Where the group has numerous statuses – as in craft hotels – the distinctions will be very clearly marked by details of dress. Once admitted into the hotel's service, the novice is stripped of his usual identity, in particular, the clothing, jewellery and personal paraphernalia by which he maintains it. What has been taken away is then replaced by a uniform of some kind, often unflattering, denoting one particular rank. If others are to interpret the actions of the new recruit correctly, it is crucial that his learner status should be openly proclaimed in this way. It will greatly ease his learning path because it will absolve him from liability for many otherwise discreditable errors which he commits during the 'make-believe' or 'not for keeps' honeymoon period. Once he abandons the learner's badge of office and achieves full status, his licence to make mistakes expires; he has entered a 'non-marginal' state and can no longer claim immunity.

Thirdly, a change of status must be accompanied by an alteration in the recruit's relationships with others. Many ethnographic accounts have recorded how the strains and tensions involved in such a change are carefully handled within a ceremonial context. Before admission to a new status is fully recognised, a candidate may be required to pass through a series of initiation tests which separate, literally, the end of one stage and the beginning of the next. While there are no real 'passing-out' ceremonies for hotel waiters, the sudden acquisition of one's own station, and the absence of a chaperone is significant enough to be recognised as a status change by co-workers.

Finally, it is worth noting that some of these processes may be so subtle as to escape the notice of the undiscerning diner, who would not know that progression from one station to another within the same establishment can alter the waiter's status significantly. So we are talking about a kind of secret society to which only the staff and perhaps a small number of the more regular clientele are admitted. How waiters learn to sidestep the pitfalls and the dangers that confront them in the course of their careers is particularly interesting in view of the fact that so little of what happens is known publicly.

RECRUITMENT AND SELECTION

In recent years the government has increased considerably the resources it devotes to the hotel and catering industry and especially in attempts to aid its difficulties in recruitment – despite current high unemployment. There are two specialist Jobcentres in London, while in the rest of the country twenty Jobcentres have specialist catering sections.

The use of Jobcentres varies widely, with their services being more demanded in the South and South East where most hotels are concentrated. Recruitment also occurs through private employment agencies, by advertisements in the trade press, in national and local newspapers and in magazines. Managers on the whole, however, always prefer to recruit through personal contact where this can be arranged, preferring their own grapevine or those of their staff to agencies or advertisements. National Economic Development Office figures (1975a, pp. 17–21) show that 42 per cent find their jobs informally through a relative or friend or through speculative enquiry.

The use of the grapevine is considered particularly preferable for senior posts and especially for such posts in higher class establishments. There is indeed a widespread suspicion at this level about advertisements. As a head waiter in Hotel 3 put it:

> if they have to advertise it, you can always bet it can't be much good!

Few managers employ inexperienced staff by choice. This means that most people entering the industry have – like Nicod – to bluff their way into their first job and then pick up the waiter's trade through observing others. Because of the spasmodic nature of labour shortages in this industry, managers often have no alternative but to take the first person who comes along on a trial basis, and dispense with his services later if he proves incompetent. The probationary period then becomes a means of rectifying mistakes in selection and weeding out the unsatisfactory recruit. Only managements in high-level hotels can rely upon a steady stream of labour at all times. Here the process of selection is tightly structured – and operates, on the whole, through routine bureaucratic procedures.

LEARNING THE ROPES

Until the recruit has acquired the knowledge and skills he requires for the job, he will be expected to behave strictly according to the existing rules. Closely connected with Goffman's notion of 'role distance' (1961, p. 82) is the ritual prescription that the novice must demonstrate 'competence, sincerity, and awareness of his place'; only then is he permitted to depart from the strict-rule role that he is officially required to play and develop strategies for corner-cutting or adopt a more individual style of working. One manager in Hotel 5 astutely likened the process to that of a person learning to drive a car:

> It's no good pretending that you know how to drive; you've got to be taught the proper way to do things at first. Once you've passed the test, you can begin to bend the rules a little, but you've got to know when things have to be done properly, and when they don't.

95

>There are times when you've always got to do things the proper way, and there are times when it doesn't matter.

Typically, then, the novice is normally taught at first to treat all the rules as unbreakable. Not until he becomes more fully socialised will he be able to distinguish which are the *general* rules, always applicable, and regulating the main part of his job; and which are *discretionary* rules, not applicable in every case, but situation-specific and associated with particular aspects of the job. In short, the course upon which he embarks becomes, over time, progressively infused with the 'moral' aspects of his career. By 'moral', we mean anything to do with a career that impinges on the individual's view of himself, but that lies outside the formal and explicit rules which limit individual autonomy. Though in fact the progression involves a gradual awakening to the moral aspect of his role, analytically both sets of rules are important to the process.

First, then, there are the general, or 'house' rules which spell out the main conduct requirements, for example, to do with the allocation of specialist tasks; workers' personal appearance, and their use of the hotel and its facilities. Upon entry, the recruit must adopt the new set of prerogatives which house rules assign him. Essentially, this is the organisation's way of initiating him into the subservient role that the service relationship necessarily implies. But as the nature and extent of these prescriptions vary considerably according to a waiter's rank, it is clear that they have a secondary purpose which we cannot ignore: that of reinforcing the internal authority structure.

Let us start with the question of work allocation. Between hotels there is quite a difference in the number of work roles that are precisely defined. In the low-level northern hotels studied, only four emerged clearly – the general manager, the restaurant manager, the head waiter and the waiter – very little remains of the ranking system which once existed (at one time each hotel had three or four ranks below the level of the present-day waiter). Interestingly enough, both hotels have retained the rank of commis, although it appears to be no more than a device to pay people less to do the same job as the waiter. The commis and the waiter wear the same uniform and, while initially the commis' duties are limited, say, to serving children (children's lunch or tea) where plate service rather than silver service is required, or to helping the waiter (known as 'vegging' because the commis serves vegetables but not meat) it is not long before he has his own station. Often, in fact, the only difference is that a commis does not have quite so many tables. As one 17-year-old, a commis in Hotel 2, put it:

> When you're asked to serve a station yourself for the very first time, it's a bit frightening. I remember feeling a little proud of myself at first. But you soon realise that there's nothing to it really and, after you've done the job for a little while, you begin to think: 'Why don't I get paid the same wage?' If you ask me, it's slave labour – and it really pisses me off that others are getting paid more to do the same job.

By contrast, in the high-level London hotels we studied, there are a large number of status differences and specialist tasks. Workers in these hotels are strongly stratified; their roles are interdependent, highly specialised, well publicised through dress, and subject to a strong element of supervisory control. A general decline in trade over the past two decades has led to a reduction in the number of staff and some changes in the system of ranking: now, instead of four or five waiters per station, the number in both hotels has dropped to two or three. Much of the old tradition still remains, however, at least compared with the vast majority of hotels which have suffered a similar falling-off of trade. Both hotels have retained the rank of commis – and those employed in this position really do have a separate function: to prepare the *mise en place*, fetch and carry food from the kitchen, clear away dirty dishes, clean down the tables, throw away leftover food and carry dirty dishes into the kitchen. The chef de rang and the station head waiter lay the tables, reheat the hot dishes, prepare salads and cold dishes, actually serve the food and generally administer the

97

customers' needs. In addition, the station head waiter normally takes the customers' orders, answers their queries about the menu, supervises the work of his staff, assists with their training, handles all the awkward customers and deals with any complaints that arise.

This brings us to the question of personal appearance. An individual normally expects to have some control over what he wears and how. But for those who work within or otherwise belong to a 'total institution' (Goffman, 1961, p. 51), the degree of control permitted will be greatly circumscribed. In many hotels, a restaurant manager used to carry out a regular tour of inspection – with all his staff lined up outside the restaurant door, their hands held out for him to examine – and anyone not having a tidy appearance or clean finger-nails faced instant dismissal. So, too, a waiter used to be denied all forms of personal adornment – such as rings, bracelets, fancy cuff-links and wrist watches – because he was supposed to be distinguished only by the rank of uniform he wore. Nowadays the rules are not so strict and not all hotels invoke the same controls. But the more prestigious the hotel, the more restrictions we find; the greater the distance between those serving and the served, the less individual autonomy the server is permitted. Before entry into the highest level hotel studied, a prospective recruit is scrutinised by the restaurant manager to find out if he possesses any disqualifying physical features: long or dirty finger-nails, long hair, hunched shoulders, poor posture, general untidiness, and the like.

In this hotel the military model was commonly used by waiters to describe the way in which the strict-rule role was imposed. One chef de rang complained:

> Three years ago, I came from Turkey to work here. I left to join the Turkish army and now I'm back again doing the same job as I did before. I didn't want the same job, but this was all I could find. Not that I'd mind so much if I wasn't told what to do all the time ... It's worse than the Turkish army for discipline.

And the second head wine waiter, who had served in the British army, used the same analogy when explaining to Nicod how he was expected to behave:

> As a waiter, you're not paid to ask questions; it's just like the army. I'll never forget that phrase we used to hear all the time I was doing military service: 'If it moves – salute it; if it doesn't – paint it.' It's the same here. If you get too big for your boots, they'll soon bring you down a peg.

PRIMARY ADJUSTMENT: ACCEPTING ONE'S PLACE

All organisations invoke controls which deny people full individual autonomy. No waiting staff are permitted to sit, eat, smoke, shout, swear, or engage in activity considered inappropriate in the customers' presence. Thus, however strong the individual's personality, the formal arrangement whereby he must always observe such rules necessitates a conscious restriction of individuality. No one can achieve this without a degree of unease. It is only when he begins to take part in the activity of the organisation *without* feeling alienated that he is transformed – that he begins to accept that self-curtailment is a 'normal', 'standard' and 'built-in' part of the job. This, in Goffman's terms, is the stage at which it is possible to speak of the individual having a 'primary adjustment' to the organisation – the point at which 'he is officially asked to be no more and no less than he is prepared to be, and obliged to dwell in a world that is in fact congenial to him' (1961, p. 172).

One way in which managements help their staff to pass through this stage is by holding parties for special festive events. Perhaps once or twice a year staff are able to engage freely in all the activities they are normally denied, and workers and management mix in a relatively relaxed and informal manner – eating and drinking together, playing party games, and talking to one another as if they were social equals. Normally such importance is attached to maintaining social distance that workers are not allowed to mingle with guests, even when off duty and out of uniform. Therefore, if a waiter wishes to eat out or celebrate, say, a wedding, or birthday, he must go outside the hotel in which he works. Inevitably this raises difficulties for the management when they try to stage a staff party. In the larger hotel a backroom or banqueting hall can be set aside for such purposes. Alternatively, hotels frequently have reciprocal arrangements so staff can be transferred to an entirely different setting whenever parties are held.

In form, a staff party is characterised by an abandonment of the formalities and the task orientation that normally govern staff/management contacts and the usual chain of command. This represents 'role release' (Goffman, 1961, pp. 90–3). At such times workers have the licence to 'take liberties' and generally act above their station, possibly imagining for a few hours that the whole world lies at their feet. In particular they are likely to cut across the system of ranking by certain standard devices.

First, the personal status of the staff is elevated because they have been granted the privilege of not wearing uniforms. As Nicod prepared to join the staff Christmas party in Hotel 3, the restaurant manager said to him: 'Don't forget to change, you want to look like a human being don't you?'; he found that staff generally obtained satisfaction from the feeling, however illusionary, that if they put on a three-piece suit they would suddenly acquire the same status as the general manager.

In some cases the staff-management line may be crossed through ritual role reversal. Essentially this means that management wait on tables for staff and perform other menial services for them (cf. Gluckman, 1955, pp. 109–36). Sometimes staff take advantage of the moratorium that exists on such occasions to say things not ordinarily permitted in order to make management feel uncomfortable. A few people will always seize the opportunity of role release to criticise, abuse, ridicule, embarrass, humiliate, or otherwise behave offensively towards management. In Hotel 3, for example, a commis chef went up to the general manager at the staff Christmas party and publicly declared: 'Mr Brown, I think you're a fucking snob!' No penalty followed because the manager was quite powerless to do anything: it is generally regarded as outside the manager's jurisdiction to punish anyone for taking advantage of the situation.

The staff party allows people this freedom to vent feelings of anger, resentment, or disrespect without fear of retribution, and, in effect, provides a safety-valve, because potentially explosive situations can thus be averted without risk of major consequences. Rather than breaking down formalised authority, such ritual role reversal buttresses it: by being allowed to break the rules on one day a year, people implicitly recognise the importance of rules for the rest of the year. Such behaviour is common in occupational cultures that emphasize strong divisions of rank as in the armed forces and among hospital staffs.

SECONDARY ADJUSTMENTS: APPRECIATING THE LITTLE THINGS

This brings us to what Goffman has called 'secondary adjustments', practices that do not directly challenge management but allow staff 'to obtain forbidden satisfactions or to obtain permitted ones by forbidden means' (1961, p. 56). Secondary adjustments might simply involve being permitted the more trivial aspects of prescribed conduct such as never smiling in the restaurant (an act for which Nicod was reprimanded in Hotel 4). For the novice these discretionary rules always apply not so much to put him in his place, but to make him fully aware, and appreciative, of the minor privileges he can gain later on.

However much the social barrier between servant and master appears to have been lifted in our society generally, we find in reality that those providing a service are still not expected to enter freely into transactions. Typically, the waiter is someone who is present, but whom others treat as if he were really not there – as if he were a 'non-person'. In its most extreme form – our highest level London hotel, for instance – this means that a waiter must not be seen eating, drinking, smoking, sitting, talking, burping, farting – or anything else which signifies being human. During his first few weeks as a commis in this hotel, Nicod continually received instructions which brought this home:

101

> Remember, Boy, while you're in the restaurant, never pick your
> nose, scratch your hair, stroke your chin, touch or put your hand
> anywhere near your face . . . and always try to stand with your back
> straight like Prince Charles!

As the carver in Hotel 4 nicely put it: 'We're only allowed to
breathe on our day off.'

Against this stark background, a small number of privileges –
which are offered in exchange for personal loyalty towards management, professional expertise, length of service, dependability,
experience and social finesse – assume immense importance. Many
of these are little more than a permit to do something that people
outside the organisation take for granted. Normally, a person
probably chooses unthinkingly when he wants to sit down,
whether he should eat or light a cigarette, or when to talk; for a
waiter such matters are problematic. Very often the need to
conceal from customers anything which contradicts the non-
person role is met by a simple expedient – a 'back region' or
'backstage' where behaviour which might conflict with the role
may be indulged. Goffman (1959a, p. 140) has defined a back
region or backstage 'as a place relative to a given performance,
where the impression fostered by the performance is knowingly
contradicted as a matter of course.' Most hotels have clearly defined
areas, often located close to the customers but cut off from their
view by a partition or guarded passageway. It is in this refuge that
the waiter can relax; he can do things in private that he is forbidden
to do in public; he can sit and chat with co-workers; he can even
engage in the illicit practice of taking food intended for the
guests. It is here that illusion created for the customers is openly
shattered, and the waiter can be a full person.

In Hotel 3, for instance, every night there was a sudden
transformation 'backstage' as soon as the time came round for the
cabaret, because service was suspended for the duration of the
show. First head waiters, wine waiters, station head waiters and
commis waiters would all rush to the various corners of the hotel in
which food had been stored for safe-keeping. They would return

with a prawn cocktail, smoked salmon, Parma ham, cold chicken, a wide range of sweets, salads, cheeses, and so on; sit on a chair or on empty upturned wine crates in a back room or just outside the wine waiter's office; and calmly munch their way through a whole meal made up of their illicit takings. No one seemed to object to this practice, so long as it was done discreetly and no tell-tale signs were left. In the words of the restaurant manager:

> Just take whatever you want. Provided I don't see you taking it, I don't really care. But once you've finished, don't forget to pick up the crumbs and clear away the dirty dishes. We'll all be in trouble if Mr Brown (general manager) sees a mess.

Obviously, if a good impression is to be maintained, the back region must be closed to those being served. Little wonder, then, that the occasional customer who wanders in, absent-mindedly, or perhaps defiantly to make a complaint, is hustled out before he is able to see anything which might shock him. It is hard to match the description of the sheer squalor that may sometimes be found hidden behind the green baize door, provided by George Orwell (1933, p. 60):

> It was amusing to look round the filthy little scullery and think that only a double door was between us and the dining-room. There sat the customers in all their splendour – spotless tablecloths, bowls of flowers, mirrors and gilt cornices and painted cherubim; and here, just a few feet away, we in our disgusting filth. For it really was disgusting filth. There was no time to sweep a floor till evening, and we slithered about in a compound of dirty water, lettuce-leaves, torn paper and trampled food. A dozen waiters with their coats off, showing their sweaty armpits, sat at the table mixing salads and sticking their thumbs into the cream pots. The room had a dirty mixed smell of food and sweat. Everywhere in the cupboard, behind the piles of crockery, were squalid stores of food that the waiters had stolen. There were only two sinks, and no washing basins, and it was nothing unusual for a waiter to wash his face in the water in which clean crockery was rinsing. But the customers saw nothing of this. There were a

coconut mat and a mirror outside the dining-room door and the waiters used to clean themselves up and go in looking the picture of cleanliness.

In most hotels access to the building from the outside is governed by the same principle. Usually, the front of the hotel building looks well decorated, well repaired and tidy; the rear is relatively unprepossessing, and is often littered with rotting garbage, dirty linen, delivery vans, cleaning equipment, unfinished brickwork and the like. Correspondingly, the customers enter through the front and the socially stigmatised – chambermaids, chefs, waiters, porters, delivery men – enter through the rear.

Such differences are familiar and obvious. Territorial arrangements, however, are not always so easy to define. Often it is not entirely clear to new staff, particularly in medium-status hotels, which areas are always strictly out of bounds to them except when on duty. Frequently it is not until *after* the rule has been broken that prohibited areas are pointed out to them. Nicod was warned by the restaurant manager in Hotel 1 after he had been there for one week: 'Mr Hamilton (duties manager) saw you sitting in the sun lounge this afternoon. Please see that it doesn't happen again, Nicod.' Then he was severely rebuked for sitting in the television room between shifts, although no one else had been present at the time. Unwittingly he had broken the house rules twice in his first fortnight. Had he not implored the duties manager to let him stay, he would have been dismissed there and then. The manager's reprimand revealed his concern not with rule-breaking per se but with the general principle if threatened:

> I'll tell you what you've done wrong. It's your whole general attitude. If you want to get anywhere in this business, my lad, you'll have to stop acting like a bloody toff. A waiter isn't expected to act like a lord; he's nothing more than a serf.

While the process of socialisation goes on, the recruit continues to receive formal and informal instruction in the 'do's' and 'don'ts'

104

of his profession. At first it must always appear that the prescriptions that limit his autonomy are much greater than those permitting him to enjoy rights or privileges, and his self-esteem is severely shaken. But as soon as he begins to learn the skills of the trade, and he is judged by others to be competent at his job, he is gradually drawn into the hotel's 'underlife' and offered a wide range of favours, privileges, forbidden satisfactions, illicit indulgences and many other forms of gratification that he is not permitted or offered access to in the early stages. Since the extent and character of this co-operation will normally be concealed and kept secret, we should expect that the novice will pass through the transition process in some furtiveness before he can begin to participate fully.

6

The Waiter's Informal Career: Learning To Be Bent

> ... Informal action may work for many ends: to change and pressure the organisation, to protect weak individuals, punish erring ones, reward others, to recruit new personnel and to maintain dignity of the formal, as well as, of course, to carry on power struggles and to work for ends we would all frown on. (Melville Dalton, *Men Who Manage*, 1959, p. 222)

Parallel with what we have termed the waiter's formal or 'basic' career, which begins when he first joins a hotel, he also embarks on a second, an informal, or, 'moral' career. This duality exists in all occupations to a greater or lesser extent: the basic career describes what is done more or less openly and the moral career is largely concerned with furtive or secret activity. This division is especially clearly marked in the case of the waiter. By becoming a hotel worker, especially if he lives on the premises, it may be argued that he chooses a life that has more in common with that of the inmates of mental hospitals, army barracks, or boarding schools than with workers in other service industries, who may be free to 'go home and forget about it till tomorrow' when the working shift ends.

Goffman has described this second career, or 'underlife', as 'the regular sequence of changes that a career entails in the person's self and in his framework of imagery for judging himself and others'. It is these that provide the 'moral' aspects of a career (1959b, p. 119). By 'moral,' then, we mean the informal side of an occupation and the effect upon the practitioner as he becomes party to it. Fiddling is part of a moral career because those who practise it have

106

undergone a moral transformation; the identity crisis marking a change of status (Becker, 1963, pp. 41–78). The basic, formal career acts as a tactical cover and public legitimation for the moral career as fiddler.

It now becomes clear that, when we use the terms 'core' and 'peripheral' to categorise waiters, we refer primarily to different stages of their moral career. 'Peripheral' workers, though apparently paid at the same rate as 'core' workers, do not substantially benefit from fiddled reward. The access to such rewards reveals a different distribution of the core and peripheral categories among different prestige hotels. Since there can be five levels involved in servicing a customer in the prestigious craft hotels, it is therefore easy to create a bureaucratic (promotional) structure for the offering of rewards. But because these levels do not exist in lower-level hotels, here rewards – no less necessary to distinguish the skilled from the unskilled – are more likely to be offered informally, in other words, through fiddles.

Little resentment is expressed over the core having the prior claim to informal rewards, however, because it is accepted as part of the perceived system of privileges for those with special skills or long service. One waiter who had worked for twenty-six years in Hotel 2, for example, was paid the same basic weekly wage as everyone else. But because he was always allocated those known to tip well, the long-stay residents and regulars, his total rewards were substantially higher than those of the other staff. No one appeared to mind. As a waitress pointed out,

> Stephan gets all the good customers, but you can't really grumble about it. When a bloke has been working in the same place for twenty-six years, he deserves a little bit extra.

Because management and core workers characteristically have considerable scope for individual contract-making, workers (particularly in the core) develop a strong sense of personal obligation towards their manager because he affords them access to fiddled benefits. It is hardly surprising, therefore, that a high labour turnover usually follows a change in management. The new

107

manager, because he knows so little about his new staff and their individual bargaining power, may try to apply general rulings which cut across the individual weightings of the informal reward system. Or he may bring in his own core workers from his past employments. Core workers, whose total rewards tend to fall most drastically under a new regime, therefore, frequently 'vote with their feet'; they often follow their old boss to his new situation or use their contacts to gain entry into the core elsewhere. This explains why there is such high personal insecurity in this industry and why it should suffer such considerable labour turnover.

This pattern of insecurity and mobility means that waiters' situations can vary dramatically – both for better or for worse. For some it can mean the sudden loss of three quarters or more of their incomes, whilst others can enjoy spectacular rises to power. Among the staff in Hotel 1, for example, it was well known that the last restaurant manager had left because he had been caught fiddling, but that now he had a job in a larger hotel further along the coast as the general manager:

> Everyone knew that the restaurant manager, head waiter, assistant general manager and a receptionist were all on the fiddle. The new general manager put a stop to it and the restaurant manager left to take a job as first head waiter at The Grand. Not long after he'd started, their general manager and the restaurant manager got the sack for fiddling . . . no one suspected him because he'd been there for such a short time – and in fact they appointed him as the new general manager! What's more, the head waiter, the assistant general manager and receptionist have all joined him at The Grand . . . and they're doing very well, thank you, so I believe. (Waitress, Hotel 1)

The Informal Rewards System

Our research confirms that formal pay represents only one part of the total rewards which many hotel workers actually receive. But while some workers benefit substantially from informal and some-

108

times illegal rewards, others certainly do not. In our experience, those who do benefit do so with the collusion of management and this kind of reward can be considered to be institutionalised.

The popular press and the television news services, as well as workers and managements in this industry, have been as guilty as anyone of misleading us on this matter – in particular in their coverage of disputes in the industry to do with union recognition and unfair dismissals. These are often to do with perceived injustices in the allocation of *informal* rewards rather than with what they are presented as being about.

In spite of the hotel industry's notoriously low basic pay, efforts made over the past thirty years by the major UK trade unions to organise it have been largely unsuccessful. According to a government report (NEDO, 1975a), a mere 13 per cent of those working in hotels and catering are unionised. There have been various explanations for this surprisingly low unionism, and Mars and Mitchell have argued elsewhere (1977) that the single most important reason is that union activists are concerned to appeal primarily to the more permanent members of the workforce, many of whom are core workers. They have aimed to do so by attempting to raise their basic pay. But the unions have failed to take into account the nature and extent of informal rewards which mainly benefit core workers and which would be at risk if rewards were to be set collectively.

Like the unions, pressure groups such as the Low Pay Unit, established to highlight the plight of low-paid workers in general, only emphasise the formal aspect of people's incomes in industries such as hotels and catering. And while there may be several reasons for the Wages Council's failure to determine minimum wage levels in this industry and to achieve effective collective bargaining, it would appear largely to be because of a lack of basic understanding. As with the trade unions and the Low Pay Unit, this too can be attributed to insensitivity to variations in local labour and product markets which affect the hidden rewards paid to catering workers. Ironically, by stressing the general low level of wages in the industry, each of these bodies does a singular disservice to those who really are at the bottom of the heap, who genuinely lack the opportunity to gain informal rewards, but whose fate is obscured by a misdirected emphasis on formal pay.

Government reports have consistently stressed both the high labour turnover rates in hotels and the low wages which the industry pays its labour, without giving much attention to the value of hidden fringe benefits which underlie and obscure an understanding of both. NEDO has estimated, for instance, that of hotel and catering workers, 49 per cent of full-time adult men and 88 per cent of full-time adult women are paid below the levels which can reasonably be said to constitute low pay (1975a, p. 13). But these figures are bound to be distorted because they ignore such things as free or subsidised food and accommodation, tips, fiddles and, most particularly, other perks which unofficially accrue to the hotel worker. When it comes to analysing and interpreting the amount of rewards which people actually take home, official statistics tell us hardly anything.

Nor do we find those who have done research in the industry a great source of enlightenment, particularly about illicit earnings. For example, although Whyte (1946) did not entirely overlook the importance of tips, service charges, bonuses and other rewards, including pilferage, he concentrated largely upon the psychological satisfactions these practices offer, without considering their influence on patterns of workplace behaviour. Indeed, he made no reference to the covert system which allows one waiter more substantial benefits than another.

Bowey, on the other hand, in her study of the restaurant industry (1976), did attempt to show the relationship between the seasonal variation in tips and the level of labour turnover. She found that the fall in tips from seasonal fluctuations often resulted in staff moving from one job to another. Philip Nailon's (1978) most useful review of the practice of tipping which he sees in terms of its value as a motivator goes further still (see also NEDO, n.d.). However, if the analysis is to include those informal aspects of hotel workers' incomes which are not quite legitimate, none of the research both he and Bowey have done goes far enough.

110

In spite of the important implications they have for the pattern of workplace relations, almost all published comments on the hotel industry have coyly neglected giving data on pilferage and theft, the numbers who benefit by its practice, the range and different types of fiddled benefits and the values and attitudes associated with it. Even in the kind of study involving in-depth participant observation where knowledge of its practice could hardly be ignored, either no mention is made of the subject at all (Spradley & Mann, 1975, and Bowey, 1976) or else it is discussed in the most condemnatory way as something which 'with sufficient supervision . . . will be detected in the long run' (Whyte, 1948, p. 89). But one cannot begin to understand the normal life of waiters without an understanding of their deviance.

Techniques and Types of Fiddling

One of the most common forms of hotel pilferage is often known simply as 'knock-off'; the term refers to illicitly obtaining food or items such as soap, toilet paper, serviettes, or tablecloths that are intended for customers' use. Almost all hotel waiting staff are permitted to indulge in this type of fiddle, but the access to these rewards varies according to the class of hotel, the techniques used, and the type of worker using them. Peripheral workers mostly take only relatively inexpensive items such as soup, sweets and *hors d'oeuvre* which are left unguarded in the kitchen. Core workers, on the other hand, are likely to take more valuable items of food through informal arrangements with kitchen staff – in exchange for a drink, a lift home, money, gifts or a favour of one kind or another. Their greater degree of involvement at work allows the development of personal relationships and in many respects the goods act as catalyst, secondary to the relationships themselves (see Henry, 1978; Henry and Mars, 1978).

In most cases, knock-off is nothing more than the food which hotel staff actually consume at work. But where free meals are provided for staff, management's level of tolerance is reduced. In our second high-class London hotel, anyone caught taking food from the kitchen was charged the same amount as a customer. Some staff, however, try to turn their quasi-legitimate rights to knock-off to greater advantage by also taking home whatever they can to satisfy their families' needs – in particular, staple foods such as bread, butter, sugar, jam, cheese, cream, tea-bags, or breakfast cereals, because these can usually be taken unnoticed and transported easily. Finally, a few go still further and make a profession out of selling 'knocked-off' food: one bought steak fillets from a 'bent' chef and resold them at a profit to a cafe down the road. To avoid detection when taking booty out of the hotel, they will strap, say, a side of smoked salmon or some fillet steaks to their legs underneath their trousers. One waiter in our first high-quality London hotel helped to run two restaurants of his own with the supplies he managed to obtain in this way.

Such characters fiddling on such a scale, however, are exceptional since they run the risk, if caught, of prosecution. In Hotel 4 a kitchen worker was arrested during Nicod's employment and later prosecuted for taking a 5-gallon tin of cooking oil. As the pastry chef pointed out, this was not so much because he had taken something which did not belong to him, but because he had exceeded long-established limits without seeking social approval:

> Everyone fiddles a little in this business. In fact, you wouldn't be considered any good as a waiter if you weren't able to make a little on the side. It's something we all do from time to time, only some are not so good at it as others. A few don't know how far you should go. One thing you've got to learn is that you shouldn't be too greedy. No one is going to mind much if you take just the small things, but when you start to nick quite expensive stuff on a regular basis, as this man was doing, you can't expect the head chef or sous chef (who get paid a percentage of the profits) to stand still while you walk off with half their earnings.

'Money fiddles' is a term we use to refer to a distinct class of fiddle; it often involves similar techniques to those used to obtain food illicitly, but is quite different because it provides staff with a direct cash benefit. In the typical lounge or restaurant, the majority of money fiddles are practised at the hotel's expense, leaving the customers unaffected and unaware. Basically these fiddles involve, first, getting food and drink past a control clerk without having it logged, serving it to the customer and then pocketing payment for it. The problem for the waiter is that he is accountable for every order he presents to the kitchen or stillroom so he must try to obtain the food and beverages without an order.

One solution is to introduce items which he has purchased outside so that a profit can be made when they are sold at the hotel's higher prices. This type of fiddle is most often practised by wine waiters. At the second northern hotel we studied one such waiter regularly unloaded from his car a boot-load of wine, beer and spirits which he would sell to customers. Another way round the problem is to charge customers for food or drink obtained as knock-off. One lounge waiter who worked in the same hotel had, over several years, developed the practice of removing a gateau from the dining-room every Sunday, and selling slices of it to the unsuspecting guests in the lounge. Again this is a fiddle commonly practised by wine waiters who, for instance, pour the left-over wine from people's bottles into a carafe which they then sell as 'house-wine'.

The most common fiddle is for waiting staff to form an alliance – with either kitchen staff, the restaurant manager, or a control clerk – which provides the access and support they need for practising undetected pilferage. As already mentioned, the kitchen staff may be bought off, granted favours, or otherwise persuaded to provide access to food for a waiter's knock-off. This food can then be sold to hotel guests who are charged the normal price for it. The chef or kitchen staff who collude with waiting staff receive a percentage of the illicit takings – usually on a 50/50 basis.

Beating the control clerk often involves considerable ingenuity especially in creating ambiguity over dockets – the carbon copies or duplicates of customers' bills. This of course is increasingly difficult to achieve now that accounts are becoming computerised.

113

Nonetheless these traditional methods are still widespread at the time of writing:

(a) Writing can often be made deliberately ambiguous. For example, fives can be made to look like threes; the customer accepts the five; the clerk accepts the three.

(b) Waiters often have a 'spare' docket book.

(c) If the waiter can retrieve the copy docket passed to the checker's desk after she has received it, this can then be re-used. One method involves the use of a wet tray placed on top of the docket which then sticks to its underside when the tray is moved. Another is to distract the clerk; an accomplice waiter, for instance, can cause an argument. A third involves different varieties of 'bending' the checker, ranging from bribery and flattery to subtle deception.

(Mars, 1973)

Even though they are aware of much of what goes on, higher management is normally outside this fiddle system. But the more lucrative dining-room fiddles do involve one or more waiters in some kind of alliance with the restaurant manager or head waiter, who facilitate pilferage and offer some protection against higher management if anything goes wrong. As Mars (1973, p. 207) has pointed out elsewhere, 'access' and 'support' always appear to be necessary for pilferage to occur: 'It is in the distribution of these two facilities and the alliances which follow such distribution that a system can be seen.'

By and large, restaurant money fiddles primarily involve the waiter pocketing the cash paid by customers for the food and service they receive. As Nailon (1978) has pointed out in the case of tipping, the manager's allocation of customers to stations may be crucial. Similarly, in the case of fiddles, by manoeuvring non-residents who are called 'chance' customers to a particular station, a head waiter is able to channel fiddled benefits to the waiter of his choice. This is why head waiters are often so insistent about where it is that customers should sit. Whereas residents usually pay for their meals by cheque at the end of their stay and are

114

therefore not good for tips or for fiddles, most chance customers pay cash to the waiter serving them.

Sets of tables which customers are most likely to find attractive, such as those near a window with a view, or those away from the clatter and smell of the kitchen, are desirable to a waiter intent on maximising income, both from tips and from fiddles. The waiter who is allocated these tables is being shown favouritism by the restaurant manager, whose strategy is neccessarily to provide his core workers with the best stations. In return for 'kick-backs', the head waiter or restaurant manager services his chosen stations in such a way that their waiters' earnings can be maximised to their *mutual* benefit.

When a party of chance customers has been steered towards a chosen table there is then a need to ensure that they choose dishes that are not normally checked by the control clerk. This is why a waiter will be likely to say: 'I can personally recommend the roast beef, sir' – or alternatively why he might eulogise over the saddle of lamb. Both dishes are normally served off the joint. They are, therefore, already in the dining room and have already bypassed the control clerk. Since control is only effected over main courses the waiter who can pull this trick can usually 'knock' the cost of the whole meal. This too, however, is a tactic that will become increasingly threatened by the growth of electronic accounting.

However, those with the greatest opportunities for money fiddles are the bar staff and wine waiters. As well as the simpler forms of pilferage, such as overcharging and short-changing, they are able to engage in a wide range of complex and lucrative fiddles, usually at the expense of the customer, not the hotel. Most involve trying to short-measure, or to pass off cheaper beer, wine or spirits as the more expensive kind ordered by the customer, and pocketing the difference in price. A waiter, for instance, who receives an order for bottled beer can usually get away with serving an ordinary draught beer which costs less. Similarly he can pour cheap wine into a bottle bearing the label of a more expensive one. Or, if he receives an order for an orange juice, he can easily get it from the

115

supply kept on tap in the kitchen but charge the customer the full price of a more expensive bottle of, say, Britvic orange.

Some of the best known and most frequently practised bar fiddles are at banquets. For example, if a table orders twelve bottles of wine, only eleven bottles may actually be served. The larger the numbers involved, the greater the ambiguity and the greater the likelihood of fiddles. Another common fiddle in bars is to water down the spirits so that the number of measures from each bottle is higher than the hotel expects, so that the extra takings can be pocketed. Alternatively, if a waiter receives an order for, say, two gin and tonics, he can pour a single measure into two glasses, and then conceal the fact by adding more tonic than usual. Or he can merely smear the brim of a glass with gin which gives the false impression of a full measure.

Finally, the night porter has his own brand of fiddles, some of which are related to the restaurant. His duties include serving sandwiches and drinks after normal hours; booking in guests who have arrived late; locking up, and keeping a watchful eye on the building. He can, of course, engage in the lounge fiddles already described, and indeed, because he often holds keys providing access to all the food or drinks in the hotel and no other staff are normally present when he is on duty, the problem of getting past the control system hardly applies. On top of this, of course, a night porter can engage in other kinds of fiddles related to room-letting: he can often earn an appreciable income by providing accommodation to prostitutes in return for a percentage of their earnings; provide prostitutes for customers, and rooms for both staff and friends to engage in their particular peccadilloes.

The enormous range of fiddles we found have a common feature: they are acts of dishonesty which the people involved do not consider dishonest. What underlies this notion is an unwritten code, not easy to discern: it sets out the limits beyond which it is considered inappropriate for a particular person in a certain situation to benefit from fiddling. This is why tacit understandings and double dealings between management and staff are necessarily complex. As a wine waiter in an extremely prestigious hotel put it, when questioned by the restaurant manager about the loss of a bottle of wine and a corkscrew belonging to a party of VIP customers:

> Well, you know that I nick things. I know that you know that I nick things. But I don't nick things when it's someone important: or, if I do, I make bloody sure that no one knows that something has been nicked!

Learning to Fiddle

Once the recruit has reached the stage when he is judged sufficiently competent to cope with the technical side of the job, it is not long before he can begin the preliminary stages of fiddle training. First of all, he may be put through a series of initiation tests to ensure successful fiddler transformation. The aim is to find out whether he is sufficiently able and willing to practise the fiddle before he is allowed to become totally involved himself. Moral training generally involves running a whole gauntlet of Hiawathan trials. Polsky, for instance, admits that, during his study of an American delinquent boys' home, he, a 6-foot 6-inch adult, only began to be tolerated as a participant-observer after a long period of testing in which, among other things, he was coerced to smoke marijuana (Polsky, 1962). Entry into the deviant subculture of hotels tends to start in a similar way with hoops for the novice to jump through that progressively draw him into his fiddler role.

Managerial hand-outs, usually consisting of a small sum, 50p for instance, are given to selected members of staff in private. This may alternatively be seen as 'hush money' or 'conscience money'. For example, when the restaurant manager in Hotel 2 received a £20 tip which the customer asked him to share with the pastry chef, he gave £1 each to the two waiters who had been standing nearby at the time. This was designed first to appease the two waiters who might have resented not getting some reward themselves; and secondly to draw them into the guilt of keeping the pastry chef's share of the money. Thus, what Cressey (1971) calls a 'non-shareable problem' emerges because in effect it seals everyone's lips and prevents the injustice coming to light.

During the initial stages the novice is largely left to pick up fiddling techniques for himself. Information about fiddling tends to be transmitted unintentionally, often imperceptibly and through a gradual process of absorption. However, if judged to have the special skills or qualities required, the recruit may be given formal instruction; in other words, demonstrations. Judgement of a recruit's character and ability is made along the lines that Sutherland observed – ideally he should have 'an adequate equipment of wit, front, talking ability . . . reliability, nerve and determination' (1937, p. 213). Self-interest or opportunism normally determine the actual occasion on which tutelage begins: a head waiter may require collaboration to obtain knock-off, provide an alibi, prevent his getting caught, or give him some kind of assistance.

At first the pupil will receive instruction in minor fiddles or quasi-legitimate perks. Once waiters are confident that a recruit has the right predisposition, they may test him out with an offer or request for something small, say, an *hors d'oeuvre* or soup. In his study of bakers' roundsmen, Ditton observed that this often took the form of a particularly loaded question – the 'alerting phrase': 'Classically between sales and bakery staff, the "alerting phrase" for "those in the know" is the demand for, or offer of, "extra bread"'. He notes that this appears in the form of a question: 'Is there any bread about?' (1977, p. 107). Similarly, Henry found that illicit trading began with what members described as either a 'test line' or a 'probe line', requesting or offering 'cheap goods', 'cheap gear', or 'cheap stuff' (1978, pp. 38–9).

It is not until the novice has shown that he has no moral qualms, and can carry out trivial acts of dishonesty satisfactorily, that he begins to become involved in more lucrative illicit activity. And before he knows what has really happened, the novice has undergone a complete 'transformation'. By this we mean an alteration of character caused 'whenever one aim grows so stable as to expel definitely its previous rivals from the individual's life' (James,

1902/1979, pp. 108–9) – the sudden realisation that one is somebody new.

Nicod's experience in Hotel 3 is a good example. One night the station head waiter approached him and asked if he would like to invite two friends for a cheap meal. His proposition was that if they shared the price of a *table d'hôte* meal between them, both could order whatever they wished from the *á la carte* menu. In order to avoid detection, an order for the *table d'hôte* meal would be placed with the chef. If questioned about the second person at the table, the waiter would simply claim that he had been taken ill and had consumed nothing at all. To obtain the second person's meal, another order with a different table number would be placed. The waiter would say, if asked, that it had been necessary to serve someone a second meal because he had complained about the first. There was no strict control on the *hors d'oeuvre* or sweets: only a few words in the ear of the cold larder or pastry chef were needed, and anything on the menu could be obtained. Once Nicod had accepted this proposition, it was not long before he was given the opportunity to try it out. Having demonstrated that he was a capable accomplice and not averse to the fiddle, he began to get drawn into the fiddle system before the significance of the situation became really clear to him.

It is useful in this connection to cite the experience of a commis chef we talked to. On the day after his arrival, he found himself being 'dragged' into deviant activity at the hotel where he worked. He simply had no choice but to take a box of After Eight chocolates which were offered him:

> They keep these chocolates in a cupboard off the dining-room and one of the assistant chefs just shoved these two boxes of After Eights at me on my second day. 'Here you are', he said, 'they're yours.' When I said I didn't want them, didn't even like the taste, he got quite firm and insisted. 'In any case, they can't be put back', he said, 'because the cupboard is locked and the record has already been altered.' Then one of the other chaps came round and got his share, and it was suggested that I couldn't really keep out of it – not without dropping some others in it, so I said 'Thank

you' and took them. After you have become involved like this,
you're trusted.

At first, then, involvement in the fiddle converts the newcomer,
whose moral attitudes are unknown and therefore 'dangerous', into
a participant, while, at the same time, providing a means to
demonstrate and reaffirm the shared culture of pilferage and the
social function which it serves. Then, as the novice begins to
practise the fiddle himself, he will rely more upon the advice
meted out to him by more experienced hands; he will obtain
greater returns, built up greater trust with his immediate super-
iors and develop the strategies required to assure success and avoid
getting caught. For instance, after two or three weeks' careful
tutelage, Nicod was advised by his station head waiter in Hotel 3
on what *types* of knock-off to take home:

> Food can be taken without much risk because as soon as you get
> home you can eat the bloody stuff, but never take china, table-
> cloths, napkins or cultery – especially if the name of the hotel is
> printed on them. You never know when they might catch up with
> you.

Sooner or later, somewhere along this chaperoned route, fiddle
occasions begin to lose their mystery and become defined as
ordinary. So, too, when the waiter's moral training is concluded,
his commitment to the wider organisation begins to fade. Instead
he develops a strong attachment to his immediate superior upon
whom he has come to depend for access to customers and goods.
But because the nature and extent of his fiddled benefits are
normally determined by the position he holds within the group,
no one worker can act individually. If he does so, he may find
himself quickly earning the scorn and contempt of co-workers; he
may even risk being reported to the police, as happened in the
cooking-oil case mentioned earlier. Only core workers can step
outside the limits and not risk having group sanctions applied
against them. This is why, despite a reputation for stealing things,
the greatest fiddler in Hotel 2 not only escaped punishment but

was promoted to night manager; although still only eighteen, he had worked in the hotel for four years and was easily the most experienced member of staff – and someone who could always be relied upon in an emergency.

The Fiddler's Culture

The focus of our interest so far has been on fiddling as a means of obtaining informal rewards that denote prestige, as part of a waiter's basic training and as compensation for low basic pay. Our broader aim is to relate the extent and nature of fiddles in different hotels to their style of management – a point more fully developed in the following chapter. However, we should not overlook the culture aspect of fiddling. Being part of a fiddle system involves taking a share in the collective responsibility for ensuring that it operates efficiently and does not exceed the level management regards as acceptable. Such involvement reinforces an individual's sense of occupational solidarity. In addition, risk-taking helps to alleviate the boredom of the job. The following comments of an assistant chef in a medium-sized, privately owned, hotel underline both of these secondary functions of fiddling.

> Most of the fiddles involve collaboration – they have to, because more than one person is usually involved. That is how you get brought into it . . . how you *have* to be brought in, in fact. Where you get a single individual responsible, then here you usually don't get fiddles. I remember a chef who stopped me nicking some salmon. 'Hey', he said, 'don't take that. I'm the only one on. I'll carry the can.'
> There's a lot of fun in hotels, and some of it has to do with fiddling. Now here's a thing I can't understand: everyone in this place seems to steal oven-cloths. It's ludicrous really; it's always done in public, it's well known about. You find people with thirty or forty oven-cloths hoarded away, and people trying to steal them off each other. And this is a funny thing, too, it's not an expensive item.

When you're stuck on the premises you really do have to fool about, there's not much else to do. So some of the fooling around you get is because for many of the staff the hotel isn't only the place they work in, it's also their home.

In every society certain individuals will be excluded from full participation because they are discriminated against in some way. Hotels are no exception, as our informant perceptively, and rather sadly, confirmed:

> There's always something wrong with chambermaids, especially the old ones. In fact, quite a few of them go potty. I suppose their trouble really is that they've got nothing to exchange.

Individual rivalries arise from the competitive striving which develops as waiters (and chefs) jockey for individual contracts in the pursuit of increased total rewards. But much of the work in hotels and restaurants – whether legitimate or otherwise – also requires collaborative support. This is why exchanges are important and why those staff with 'nothing to exchange', like chambermaids, tend to be excluded from social involvement.

This informant's account also gives us a clue to understanding what lies behind the oven cloth episodes he refers to. Here we have an example of group involvement in play. The episodes serve to emphasise and develop a group identity that can – and on occasions must – override competitively derived individual rivalries (see also Roy, 1954). Oven cloths, therefore, became invested with internal symbolic value in this particular restaurant precisely because they had no external (and therefore divisive) exchange value.

In other restaurants different forms of collective involvement arise but the need, however, is always to emphasise in-group identity, which, especially among waiters in lower level hotels, is otherwise threatened by divisions over the allocation of stations, chance customers and particularly the access to fiddled benefits. Where, however, extensive total rewards are allocated only to a small elite core, as in the higher level hotels we studied, then here we find no ambiguity over who is trying to get what, and therefore no conflicting rivalries that need to be smoothed over before minimum cooperation can exist.

The non-spectacular way in which people become involved in deviant activity has a number of functions. One is to provide the kind of training required without fear of arousing the management's suspicion and, at the same time, without exposing the recruit to unnecessary risks: in addition, of course, because anyone who does not accept the fiddle poses something of a threat to those who practise it, teaching the moral career in stages makes it possible to identify the whistle-blowers before they have the chance to report a major fiddle. Thus, teaching recruits the rudiments of the fiddler's craft in stages has a purely practical function.

But the gradual progression involved in teaching a recruit to be bent serves a second function: it helps to soften the emotional blow that sudden awakening to a fiddler role might cause. No identity crisis or 'psyching out' (Davis, 1968, pp. 244–5) is experienced until after the novice has learnt the techniques and practised their use. By this stage the learner has become a fully fledged fiddler. Thus he turns into someone who can be trusted because he is 'one of us' – being no longer a 'marginal man' (Hughes, 1958, p. 120) but someone as strongly committed as 'we' are. Hence a third function is that direct involvement in deviant activity amounts to a *permanent* transformation – it is a loss of virginity. Once the novice begins to practise the art of fiddling himself, there can be no return to his previous state of innocence. However insignificant this might seem, the act is irreversible and changes people for ever (see Becker 1963 pp. 31–9). Once a fiddler, always a fiddler, we might say.

7

Hotels: A New Classification and Its Implications

Grid/Group Analysis

We have found that the hotel industry can best be understood in terms of the constraints affecting the behaviour of their staff and customers – and of how they perceive the world. People everywhere build up their own distinct culture based on a common set of beliefs, attitudes, values, justifications and explanations. Two factors are dominant in determining people's view of the world and their workplace behaviour – both of which are to do with the structure of the work-group or organisation in which they find themselves. The first is the degree of constraint prescribing what they can do – and how far their roles are formalised; the second reflects the extent of their group involvement. These are, in fact, the central dimensions on which Mary Douglas's (1978 and 1982) ideas of 'grid' and 'group' are based.

Grid refers to the total body of rules and constraints which a culture imposes on its people in a particular context; in this case, they prescribe what the individual can do in the workplace and at his particular occupational level. *Strong grid* is associated with a precise definition of roles and statuses and a high degree of insulation, together with a lack of scope for individual autonomy and entrepreneurial activity. The Indian caste system – or any culture where social position is largely determined by 'fixed' factors such as age, sex, or birth – is a good example. By contrast, in cases of *weak grid* the invidivual is in a state of free, open, opportunist competition with others; in a system in which everything is potentially negotiable and nothing is fixed in advance. Our own culture is of this type – it places a high premium on achievable status, social mobility and competition, while the fixed factors of age, sex and birth are less important in determining social position. In fact, status is increasingly judged on merit alone, while autonomy and invididuality – the kind of characteristics associated with weak grid – are highly valued.

Group, the second dimension, refers to the extent to which an individual is morally coerced by others, through being a member of a bounded face-to-face unit; in our context, it is a measurement of the strength or weakness of people's associations with one another in the workplace. In *strong group* cultures people have a sense of belonging to a well-defined group, the survival of the group is more important than the survival of the individual and the interests of the individual are essentially subordinate to those of the group. In addition, where group is strong the individual will interact with the same people at work, during leisure, in place of abode and on family occasions. The immigrant ghetto is a good example; so are cultures that emphasise lineage and clan organisation, religious sects and other close-knit groupings. On the other hand, some cultures minimise the strength of moral coercion which groups can exert over the individual, and these are *weak on group*. This is not to say that these societies have no groups at all. There may be several groups within them but none can exert overiding control over people – these then are cultures rather like our own, especially in its urban aspects.

On one level, the grid and group classifications provide a systematic basis for defining four main types of social environment in which one might expect different degrees of control and exclusion. At another level, it is all that needs to be known for the identification of distinctive value and belief systems (cultures). Capable of expansion or reduction between macro-and micro-scale social behaviour, it is a method of analysis that can be applied to the smallest primitive society and the largest modern industrial one. Here it has been used to look at hotels. It does so from the

Figure 7.1   *Four main types of social environment*

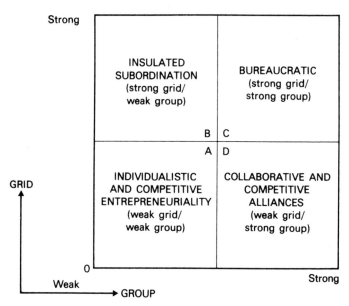

standpoint of the 'average' or typical waiter who predominates in different types of hotel restaurant.

We actually find two types of hotel worker. On the one hand, there are those for whom experiences on and off the job are quite separate: in their case there is little spillover between work and non-work activity and the values present in each are generated by different sources. Some staff, on the other hand, are attracted to the hotel industry by the cheap accommodation and the occupational environment that allows relationships to be carried over to non-work domains. For them, the hotel is a kind of 'total institution' as defined by Goffman (1961) – most notably where a high proportion of staff 'live in'.

Grid and group can be combined to produce two constructed scales independent of each other. We have applied these to predict that certain characteristics will be associated with each one. Thus if we take the five hotels studied, we can predict that differences may

126

Figure 7.2   *Classification of the five hotels studied by grid and group*

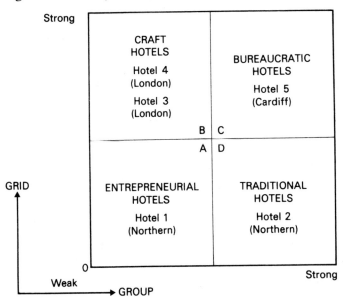

be found in such things as the control of resources, staff recruitment, staff development, workplace relations and work orientation. We have developed several hypotheses along these lines: these are arranged in the tables below under the 'area' headings, the first dealing with grid and the second with group.

Table 7.1   *Characteristics associated with grid (area A)*

Area		Strong grid (= Low personal autonomy)	Weak grid (= High personal autonomy)
A1	Total rewards system	Only the higher ranks receive a substantial element of non-taxable, non-formalised reward.	Though often having the same rank and basic pay, the core receive a substantially higher non-taxable reward than the peripheral workers.

127

A2	Control of resources	Centralised control: (a) Money: Tip-earnings collected and redistributed according to rank by the restaurant manager ('tronc')	Individual autonomy: (a) Money: Workers allowed to keep their own tips.
		(b) Food: Distribution of free food to staff controlled by establishing a canteen.	(b) Food: Each individual has to rely largely on his own ability to get food by 'knock off'.
		(c) Time: Work hours fixed in advance, overtime worked is paid; little scope for individuals to work to their own time table.	(c) Time: Work hours vary according to the time taken to complete a particular task, so work longer and overtime is unpaid – although core workers often informally rewarded; greater flexibility in organising the disposition of one's time and work routine.
		(d) Space: Individuals' control of their own set of tables is not significant, because 'tronc' is in operation.	(d) Space: Retaining the same set of tables is highly valued, and often signifies the individual's position in the informal status hierarchy.
A3	Work assessment	Rule-constrained method: assessment of workers' performance by rules fixed in advance.	*Ad hoc* approach: workers' performance judged primarily by achieving good results, whatever the means.
A4	Staff recruitment	Formal personnel procedures considered sufficient for the most part; people rarely employed on a casual basis.	Recruitment based on personal contact for the most part; casual labour often used.
A5	Career progression	Roles ascribed on the basis of age, previous experience, length of service; also roles achieved, but poor agreement between ranks on the criteria for judging successful performance.	All roles achieved on the basis of skill, speed, personal qualities (core workers often distinguished by this means alone); good agreement on the criteria for judging successful performance.

Table 7.2   *Characteristics associated with group (area B)*

Area		Strong	Weak
B1	Workplace relations	Organised group: interdependent and interchangeable roles; close co-operation both between and within ranks; considerable overlap between work and non-work relationships.	Network: clear differentiation of tasks within the workplace (Barnes 1954); some co-operation between ranks but competition and potential conflict in the same rank; separate spheres of interaction outside workplace.
B2	Work orientation	Solidaristic – collective power; work seen as an activity valued for itself; close identification with a group, with co-workers and sometimes with the wider organisation.	Instrumental – militates against collective action; work seen as the economic return for effort; involvement in the organisation only maintained for reasons of self-interest.
B3	Low collectivism	Discontent restrained by the narrow economic reference points a worker tends to adopt (Runciman, 1966); comparison with other lower paid workers masks the actual inequalities.	Resigned toleration of a low-paid and low-status job guaranteed because there is no notion of collective solidarity: labour forces are too segmented to act collectively; if discontented, individuals leave.
B4	Individual contracts	Management able to rely upon the united strength of the workforce and the individual's desire not to disappoint others in the group; individual contracts manipulated to encourage workers to remain loyal to the group (and to the management).	Management closely dependent on the availability and expertise of its core staff; individual contracts made to encourage loyalty and greater degree of obligation to the manager – weakens workers' commitment to the group.

B5	Blame- passing	Strong sense of group solidarity makes it difficult to pass blame, particularly in high-grid hotels; suspicion often covertly pinned on hidden enemies of the group if grid is weak.	No obligation to conceal hostility; blame passed frequently both between and within different sections of the workforce.

Recent Trends in the Hotel Industry

In the traditional small independently run hotel, because management-staff relations are based on a high degree of individual contract-making, there is considerable scope for individual autonomy – and those employed in such hotels tend to have an entrepreneurial attitude towards work. This echoes J. P. Henderson, whose study of the American hotel and lodging industry provides an interesting insight into the way small independent hotels are run (1965, p. 61):

> A worker who receives seventy five per cent of his income from tips is not an *employee* in the usual sense but merely a private entrepreneur doing business on somebody else's property ... it is questionable whether there is really a wage contract or whether it would not be more accurate to say the worker has merely been given permission to do business on the premises.

We contend that fiddles, knock-off and other informal additions to pay serve a similar function to tips. How well people are able to compete against others within a given grouping is important, and so are the collusive arrangements which may develop between management and staff. In effect, where individuality, competition and entrepreneuriality have a free rein, it is at the expense of group values and group solidarity. In Douglas' terms, this kind of hotel is weak grid and weak group.

With the entry of conglomerate and brewing companies into

the industry, many hotels have developed a more centralised and bureaucratic management structure, resulting in a reduction of the autonomy of both the unit manager and the rank and file worker. Instead of informal rewards, there are incremental procedures for advancement by which a worker's income steadily increases over time and largely due to rank. Work itself is organised according to a rigid breakdown of specialist functions: workroles are formally differentiated and interdependent, and stratification is aranged from above according to such criteria as age or seniority rather than personal qualities. If workers have strong feelings of loyalty towards the manager, it is because each individual gladly accepts his place and function within the organisation as part of a team – striving to achieve a common objective rather than a private end. What we find here, then, is strong group and strong grid.

There would be little need for further discussion if all large conglomerate hotels possessed the same management structure and if the trend away from the small independently run hotels could be plotted along a graph, which showed a consistent increase in specific effects on the division of labour and workplace behaviour. But while the contrast of conglomerate with small traditional hotels is basic, these are not the only forms of management structure. Indeed there are a large number of small owner-managed hotels in which individual autonomy and job discretion are rated highly, but where group influences and group commitments are also found. These are independent hotels in which a large element of the workforce 'live in', and individuals closely identify with the group, whether it is with co-workers or with the wider organisation. Here, essentially, is a context strong on group and weak on grid.

Finally, there are a small number of hotels which have a strong element of bureaucratic control but lack any sort of group support or control. Predominantly, these are the most prestigious London establishments which have a highly structured pattern of work organisation but, at the same time, generally involve people working in relative isolation. Highly personalised service demands such a complex hierarchical system that group unity is unable to flourish. At the same time, autonomy is a rare commodity – particularly in the lower ranks where people are required to accept the constraints placed upon them. Such hotels are strong on grid and weak on group.

Using the statistics gathered for *Hotel Prospects to 1985* (NEDO, 1976), we can estimate the overall distribution of hotels from now until 1990 in terms of this fourfold classification that emerges with a grid and group analysis (see Figures 9.1 and 9.2). The essential point is that hotels and catering (and probably this applies to other industries as well) should not simply be considered as a single industry in which blanket solutions can somehow be found to alleviate industrial relations problems and develop managerial policy. The implications for training, recruitment, selection, trade union representation, labour turnover and employee participation would seem to be quite different in the four categories.

Management Policy and Industrial Relations

It is our view that there are no standard management principles valid for all types of organisation and this is especially evident when we look at hotels. Though certain policies may work in a particular type of hotel, this is no guarantee that the same policies will be equally effective when applied to another type. Obviously if we can identify and develop a classification that provides a method of analysis for understanding the nature of the industrial organisation, we can at least suggest policies that *ought* to ensure success. Grid/group analysis, we have argued, can serve this purpose.

In considering the main features of the four occupational contexts our evidence assumes that these quadrants are pure or 'ideal' types. It is recognised that many organisations are not as clearly defined or definable as the schema would suggest. But it is the most extreme cases that are the most interesting and informative, and it is on these that we shall therefore concentrate our attention.

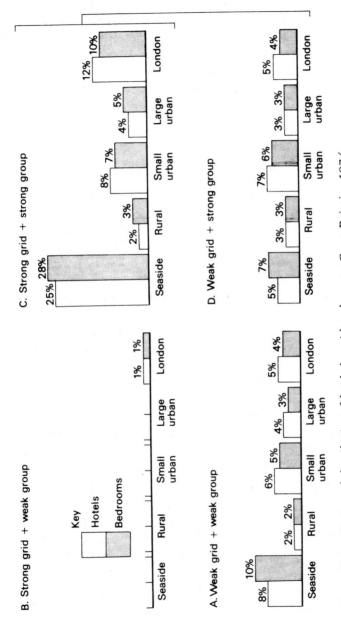

Figure 9.1   *Estimated distribution of hotels by grid and group, Great Britain, 1974*

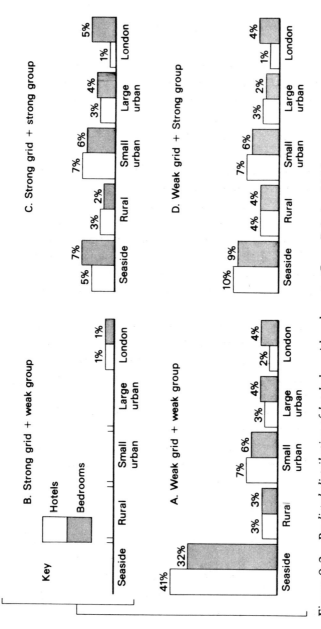

Figure 9.2 Predicted distribution of hotels by grid and group, Great Britain, 1990

THE ANALYSIS

Entrepreneurial Hotels: Weak Grid + Weak Group (Quadrant A in figures 7.1/7.2)

Description   This is the quadrant of the traditional independent hotel. Individual differences make for disproportionate returns, and flair, competition and entrepreneuriality have a free rein.

Attitudes to work   Entrepreneurial orientation. Work is seen as the economic return for effort. Involvement in the organisation is only maintained for reasons of self-interest.

Labour turnover   Core workers are the stable element, but they tend to follow their old boss to his new position because loyalty is felt towards him and not towards the organisation.

Suggested training and recruitment improvements   Competitive individual incentive schemes eliminate the need for individual contract making. An incentive example: payments to staff, as well as management, which are related to results by comparing performances with forecasts, targets, standards or budgets on an individual basis.

Unionisation   Unions are never likely to make great inroads because labour forces are too segmented and entrepreneurial to be organised on a collective basis. Their best prospect is to convince core workers of the overall advantages of a proper employment contract.

Consultation with management   No method of consultation is likely to be effective because workers prefer to vote with their feet rather than raise complaints. Employees leaving should be interviewed to discover the real reasons for their departure.

Craft Hotels: Strong Grid + Weak Group (Quadrant B in Figure 7.1/7.2)

Description   These are hotels which isolate workers and in which individual autonomy is extremely low; a very small proportion of hotels, namely, the most prestigious, fall into this category.

Attitudes to work   Cosmopolitan orientation. Employees' major reference group is *outside* the hotel: within a craft or professional

135

group (consisting of other waiters of about the same rank from the other high-prestige hotels). There is a short-term commitment only from the peripheral.

Labour turnover   Lower ranks regard their limited stay as an apprenticeship that defers greater rewards until later; this is hardly a problem for management who can always attract labour. Those holding higher office tend to stay as core workers.

Suggested training and recruitment improvements   Given that the number of higher ranking jobs are not sufficient to meet demand, there is no hope of encouraging people to stay, but the intermittent and irregular nature of their movement can be controlled through the provision of special training: off-the-job training to lessen pressure for the high standard of work at the learning stage; and also because only the rudiments tend to be taught on the job, not a thorough training – by arrangement with similar high-quality establishments.

Unionisation   Good prospect of unionisation only among stable minority of higher ranks – if attention is focused on the advantages of a formal contract rather than basic pay. Little prospect of change among low levels because of high labour turnover.

Consultation with management   All formal and informal methods of consultation likely to be avoided at all levels because it is generally felt that staff have no need to discuss complaints or policy matters (hotels renowned for their die-hard conservatism).

Bureaucratic Hotels: Strong Grid + Strong Group (Quadrant C in Figures 7.1/7.2)

Description   This is the quadrant of the large conglomerate-owned hotel, organised bureaucratically into work-groups that are highly stratified and interdependent.

Attitudes to work   Local bureaucratic organisation. Workers have a strong commitment to the organisation – work is seen as a service to it in return for steadily increasing income, social status, long-term security, incremental procedures of advancement.

Labour turnover   Lower ranks stay if provision is made for them to achieve higher position within the organisation. Those holding higher office tend to leave for higher quality establishments.

Suggested training and recruitment improvements   *All* workers should be given the same opportunities for advancement, through formal bureaucratic procedures. The danger is that the unit manager will try to operate with the same sort of informal rules traditionally found; so individual contract-making must not be allowed to interfere with the allocation of rewards. On-the-job training, which is cheaper and more effective here, will also attract and retain recruits. Movement of higher ranks can be controlled by an explicit local agreement with more prestigious hotels, who, when they require high-level staff, appoint someone from lower prestige hotels. In effect, this adds more rungs to the promotional ladder. (For details of a case study illustrating how this strategy was applied, see Mars *et al*, 1979, ch. 4.)

Unionisation   Good prospects of unionisation at all levels – if recruitment is directed towards organising cohesive and stable elements of the workforce on a local shop-floor basis.

Consultation with management   Strong preference for formal methods of consultation among the staff. There is a need for regular meetings between staff representatives, heads of departments and management to discuss complaints and the like.

Traditional Hotels: Weak Grid + Strong Group (Quadrant D in Figures 7.1/7.2)

Description   Often small independently run hotels where workers 'live in'.

Attitudes to work   Local work-group orientation. Work is seen as an activity valued in itself. Informal rewards reinforce close identification with a group, either co-workers or with the wider organisation, and also mark status within the group.

Labour turnover   Peripheral workers tend to leave (often in large numbers) for better pay and conditions elsewhere; those who stay long enough to enter the core tend to remain.

Suggested training and recruitment improvements Multi-skilling to reduce high peripheral turnover: staff with a special knowledge of one task are trained in other occupational duties, so that wider responsibilities and, therefore, satisfaction will be built into the individual's work. It allows more flexible working conditions for staff – relieves monotony and, possibly, reduces split shifts. For managements, it allows them to cope with varying demands and recruit from a wider field.

Unionisation Poor prospect of union recruitment because core staff appear to lose so much in real terms from a collective contract. Union officials tend to be regarded as 'outsiders', but with a strong local shop steward it may be possible to take advantage of the stability of core workers.

Consultation with management Informal procedures for consultation likely to be favoured by staff. Employees should be encouraged to discuss complaints directly with their immediate superior or manager.

A CLOSER LOOK AT UNIONISATION PROSPECTS

Because the majority of workers in this industry have traditionally held an entrepreneurial attitude towards their work, it is not hard to understand why trade unionism has been resisted for so long in hotels and catering. Management has been able to deter the growth of collectivism by manipulating the allocation of informal rewards in favour of its core staff. And it is these core workers who offer unions their best and most likely chance of establishing stable trade union organisation. But those who are willing to lend support to trade unions will generally be guided by considerations of the *individual* benefits that collective action might bring, and in terms of the *amount* they receive in total weekly earnings, core workers are not badly off. What they do say causes them considerable anxiety, however, is the *lack of security* that their jobs afford them. The most likely prospect for their unionisation, then, is not, as in the past, for unions to argue about basic pay but instead to focus upon the overall advantages of having a formal contract of employment.

These can be briefly summarised as follows:

1 *Holiday and sickness benefits fully guaranteed.* Hotel workers who depend on informal rewards for a large proportion of their income, face a substantial drop in wages when absent from work. They can expect to receive only their basic wage, with none of their individual-contract benefits.

2 *Protection against casual dismissal.* So long as workers must depend on illegitimate or quasi-legitimate rewards for part of their income, they will be an easy target for casual dismissal. Given that anyone caught fiddling can be dismissed, management can take advantage of the situation to eliminate those it regards as trouble-makers. One hotel chain has used this technique to dismiss emergent union organisers (Mars and Mitchell, 1977).

3 *Mortgage and cheap credit facilities.* Although core workers may substantially benefit from untaxable income, because of low (visible) wages, they are less likely to become home-owners – the best opportunity for capital accumulation that most people have. And they cannot raise a mortgage on fiddled income, so this limits the value of the property they can buy. Nor can they obtain cheap credit facilities in the same way as workers who enjoy more visible rewards.

4 *Work hours and conditions.* Because pay comprises a wide range of resources, not all of which are explicit or easily discernible, it is often difficult for an individual to equate hours worked with rewards received; there is also little effective basis for collective bargaining.

The advantage to workers of proper employment contracts coupled with a written document that specifies their duties, is that they would no longer be obliged to perform tasks or work hours unspecified in their contract – and should they be asked, they are not obliged to consent to do so. But when formal collective contracts replace individual, informal ones, their benefits are often secured at a price – the cost is the entrepreneurial flair and the

139

individualism that makes this such a lively and stimulating industry, and one able to cope with its periodic crises.

The disadvantage for managers is that they will in their turn possess less autonomy if they lose the ability to cope with ad hoc crises by no longer being able to manipulate individual contracts. The direction of change, however, is clearly set. It is epitomised by what we have called 'the ambiguous middle', those middle range hotels whose development is spearheaded by the new wave of conglomerate owners with experience and interests derived from outside the industry (Medlik, 1978, p. 229). They see advantages in increased control over their local managers and over their workforces – particulary in the nature and extent of their total rewards and especially the informal aspects of these. Centralised collective bargaining goes some way to offer them both.

Epilogue: *The Customer's Experience of Eating Out*

Eating out can, for us, never be the same again. In researching and in writing this book we have had the rare chance to explore and be involved in a secret world and to look at this world through the eyes of the natives. It is our hope to have made our explorations available to our readers.

Now when we enter a restaurant we can understand better the mystery of why we should be so firmly and carefully seated at one table rather than another: we know that we have been assessed with some finesse according to our tipping potential. We might, if we are lucky, be seen as 'good for a drop' or, if the cues we offer are unfavourable, merely as a 'mean peasant.' But we know that this rapid assessment will affect the kind of service we receive and that we are in some part responsible for the impression we make.

With knowledge, however, comes power – now we have the power to alter our situation – or at least to amend it a little. We know something of how to get the jump on the waiter – or if this is too ambitious – we can perhaps stop him getting the jump on us. And if after all he is more skilled than we are – and the chances are that he will be – then at least we can sit back, smile resignedly and appreciate his technique.

But with a gain of knowledge, we also lose something of the bliss that comes with ignorance. Never again can we accept with trusting faith the waiter's suggestion that he can particularly recommend the roast beef tonight! 'Aha', we say to ourselves, 'here we are as chance customers and the bill is about to be knocked!' The cost after all will fall on the restaurant and the benefit to the waiter – at least in his eyes is that he is earning a part of legitimate pay. And a whole hierarchy depends on him getting it.

But if we gain in power and enjoyment we do have burdens – now that we can classify our hotels and their restaurants we can understand that the ambiguous middle just cannot offer the top

141

international level of service they pretend. And at the price we pay it is perhaps churlish of us to expect it.

Above all we now know more about the waiter. We know that really his interests and ours overlap. He is not there to rob us, but to see that we enjoy the occasion. If this involves us in being just a little bit manipulated it really is for our own good. And when the time comes for us to leave our tip, we should acknowledge that a skilled waiter, like any other good craftsman, should get his just reward.

Glossary of Terms

à la carte: a menu offering unrestricted choice

chance: a customer off the street, one who has not pre-booked – or in the case of a hotel's restaurant – one who is not a resident

chef de parti: a junior ranked chef in a high class restaurant; has a wide range of tasks in food preparation; an all-purpose chef

chef de rang: not a chef, a relatively senior waiter, usually in charge of two or more junior waiters in a high class restaurant; responsible overall for serving the food and laying the tables

commis: a trainee chef or waiter. The most junior member of the waiting or kitchen staff. If a waiter, brings food from the kitchen, clears the dirty dishes; a general dogsbody

demi chef: again, not a chef; a waiter ranked just above the commis in a high class restaurant

drop: a tip – literally enough to buy a drink, used in the North of England and in Scotland: refers to a measure of whisky

extra duck: casual waiting staff recruited especially for special functions such as weddings and banquets

knock-off: pilferable items, usually considered as part of normal and expected earnings in many restaurants. Hence 'knock-off bag' – the kind of capacious shopping bag carried by women staff – often used jocularly

mise en place: one who prepares the station (see below) for the next sitting; ensures that food from the kitchen is ready for serving and generally assists the chef de rang; this includes laying the table as well as replacing any materials the waiter might need

plongeur: dishwasher; the lowest form of restaurant life

sous chef   a middle ranked chef in a high class restaurant – usually the first to receive a waiter's orders and responsible for preparing sauces

station: a group (or set) of tables

station head waiter: a senior ranked waiter in a high class restaurant, known as such because he is in charge of a station; responsible for seating customers; taking orders; handling complaints, and the maintenance of as high a level of service as possible. He usually has three or more junior waiters under his control

table d'hôte: a menu with restricted choices within a set number of courses

vegging: the serving of vegetables – one of the tasks of a commis waiter, an important part of his training

Bibliography

Barnes, A. (1954), 'Class and committees in a Norwegian island parish', *Human Relations*, vol. 7, pp. 39–58.

Becker, H. S. (1963), *Outsiders* (New York: The Free Press).

Becker, H. S., Geer, B., *et al* (eds) (1968), *Institutions and the Person* (Chicago)

Bell, D. (1974), *The Coming of Post-Industrial Society* (London: Heinemann).

Boella, M. (1974), *Personnel Management in the Hotel and Catering Industry* (London: Barrie & Jenkins).

Bowey, A. M. (1976), *The Sociology of Organisations* (London: Hodder & Stoughton).

Bradney, P. (1957), 'The joking relationship in industry', *Human Relations*, vol. 10, pp. 179–87.

Butler, S. B., and Snizek, W. E. (1976), 'Waitress-diner relationships', *Sociology of Work and Occupations*, vol. 3, no. 2 (May).

Chivers, T. S. (1973), 'The proletarianisation of the service worker', *Sociological Review*, n.s. 21, pp. 633–56

Cooper, C. L., and Oddie, H. (1972), 'Group training in a service industry: improving social skills in motorway service area restaurants', *Interpersonal Development*, vol. 3, pp. 13–39.

Cressey, D. R. (1971), *Other People's Money: A Study of the Social Psychology of Embezzlement* (Belmont Calif.: Wadsworth).

Dalton, M. (1959), *Men Who Manage* (New York: Wiley).

Davis, F. (1968), 'Socialisation as subjective experience: process of doctrinal conversion among student nurses', in Becker *et al.* (eds) (1968), pp. 244–5.

Ditton, J. (1977), *Part-Time Crime: an Ethnography of Fiddling and Pilferage* (London: Macmillan).

Douglas, M. (1966), *Purity and Danger: An Analysis of Concepts of Pollution and Taboo* (London: Routledge & Kegan Paul).

Douglas, M. (1970), *Natural Symbols: Explorations in Cosmology* (London: Barrie & Rockliff).

Douglas, M. (1972), 'Deciphering a meal', *Daedalus, Journal of the American Academy of Arts and Sciences*, vol. 101, no. 1, pp. 61–80.

Douglas, M. (1978), '*Cultural Bias*', Occasional Paper No. 34, Royal Anthropological Institute of Great Britain and Ireland.

Douglas, M. (ed.) (1982) Introduction to *Essays in The Sociology of Perception* (London: Routledge and Kegan Paul)

Douglas, M., and Nicod, M. (1974), 'Taking the biscuit: the structure of British meals', *New Society*, vol. 30, pp. 744–7.

Dumont, L. (1972), *Homo Hierarchicus: The Caste System and Its Implications* (London: Paladin).

Erikson, K. (1967), 'A comment on disguised observation in sociology', *Social Problems*, no. 14, pp. 366–73.

Fuller, J., and Currie, A. J. (1966), *The Waiter* (London: Barrie & Rockliff).

Galbraith, J. K. (1974), *Economics and the Public Purpose* (London: Deutsch).

145

The World of Waiters

Gans, H. G. (1968), 'The participant observer as human being' in Becker *et al.* (eds) (1968).

Gershuny, J. (1978), *After Industrial Society? The Emerging Self-Service Economy* (London: Macmillan).

Gluckman, M. (1955), *Custom and Conflict in Africa* (Glencoe, Ill.: The Free Press).

Goffman, E. (1959a), *The Presentation of Self in Everyday Life* (Harmondsworth: Penguin).

Goffman, E. (1959b), 'The moral career of the mental patient', *Psychiatry*, vol. 22.

Goffman, E. (1961), *Asylums: Essays on the Social Situation of Mental Patients and Other Inmates* (Harmondsworth: Penguin).

Goffman, E. (1971), *Relations in Public* (Harmondsworth: Penguin).

Hall, E. (1959), *The Silent Language* (Fawcett Publications).

Halmos, P. (1965), *The Face of the Counsellors* (London: Constable).

Halmos, P. (1970), *The Personal Service Society* (London: Constable).

Hecht, J. J. (1956), *The Domestic Servant Class in Eighteenth Century England* (London: Routledge and Kegan Paul).

Henderson, J. P. (1965), '*Labor Market Institutions and Wages In The Lodging Industry*', Bureau of Business and Economic Research, Michigan State University.

Henry, S. (1978), *The Hidden Economy: the Context and Control of Borderline Crime* (London: Martin Robertson).

Henry, S., and Mars, G. (1978), 'Crime at work: the social construction of amateur property theft', *Sociology*, July.

Hughes, E. C. (1945), 'Dilemmas and contradictions of status', *American Journal of Sociology*, vol. 50 (March), pp. 353–9.

Hughes, E. C. (1958), *Men and Their Work* (Glencoe, Ill.: The Free Press).

James, W. (1902–1979), *The Varieties of Religious Experience* (London: Fontana).

Karen, R. L. (1962), 'Some factors affecting tipping behaviour', *Sociology and Social Research*, vol. 47, pp. 68–74.

Levi-Strauss, C. (1970), *The Raw and the Cooked: Introduction to a Science of Mythology*, Vol. 1 (London: Jonathan Cape).

Lipman, A. (1967), 'Chairs as territory', *New Society*, vol. 20 (April), pp. 564–6.

Lyman, S. M., and Scott, M. B. (1967), 'Territoriality: a neglected sociological dimension', *Social Problems*, vol. 25 (Fall), pp. 243–4.

Mann, T. (1973) *Confessions of Felix Krull, Confidence Man* (Harmondsworth: Penguin)

Mars, G. (1973), 'Hotel pilferage: a case study in occupational theft', in M. Warner (ed.), *The Sociology of the Workplace* (London: Allen & Unwin), pp. 200–210.

Mars, G. (1974), 'Dock pilferage', in Rock P. and McIntosh M. (eds), *Deviance and Control* (London: Tavistock), pp. 209–28.

Mars, G. (1982), *Cheats at Work: An Anthropology of Workplace Crime* (London: Allen & Unwin).

Mars, G., and Mitchell, P. (1976), *Room for Reform: A Case Study on Industrial Relations in the Hotel Industry* (Bletchley: Open University Press).

Mars., G., and Mitchell, P. (1977), 'Catering for the low paid: invisible earnings', *Low Pay Unit Bulletin*, no. 15 (August),

146

Mars, G., Mitchell, P., and Bryant, D. (1979), *Manpower Problems in the Hotel and Catering Industry* (Farnborough, Hants: Saxon House).

Mayer, A. C. (1960), *Caste and Kinship in Central India: A Village and Its Region* (London: Routledge).

Medlick, S. (1978), *Profile of the Hotel and Catering Industry* (London: Heinemann)

Mikes, G. (1950), *Land of Milk and Honey* (London/New York: Wingate).

Miller, E. J., and Rice, A. K. (1967), *Systems of Organisation* (London: Tavistock).

Nailon, P. (1978), 'Tipping: a behavioural review', *Hotel and Catering Institute Management Association Review*, vol. 2., no. 4, pp. 231–43.

NEDO, Economic Development Committee (1975a), *Manpower Policy in the Hotels and Restaurant Industry* (London: HMSO).

NEDO, Economic Development Committee (1975b), 'Trends in catering: a study in eating out', *Quarterly Report*, no. 4 (January–March) (London: HMSO).

NEDO, Economic Development Committee (1976), *Hotel Prospects to 1985* (London: HMSO).

NEDO, Economic Development Committee (n.d.), *Why Tipping?* (London: HMSO).

Nicolson, N. (ed.) (1970), *Harold Nicolson, 'Diaries and Letters: 1937–45'* (London: Collins/Fontana).

Orwell, G. (1933), *Down and Out in London and Paris* (Harmondsworth: Penguin).

Polsky, H. W. (1962), *Cottage Six: The Social System of Delinquent Boys in Residential Treatment* (New York: Wiley).

Private Eye 6 June 1980 (London: Pressdram Ltd.)

Radcliffe-Brown, A. R. (1965), *Structure and Function in Primitive Society* (New York: The Free Press).

Riesman, D. (1950), *The Lonely Crowd* (Yale University Press)

Roy, D. F. (1959), 'Banana Time', *Job Satisfaction and Informal Interaction* (Human Organisation), Vol. 18, part 4, pp. 158-68.

Runciman, W. G. (1966), *Relative Deprivation and Social Justice* (Harmondsworth: Penguin).

Selltiz, C., Jahoda, M., Deutsch, M., and Cook, S. W. (1969), *Research Methods in Social Relations* (London: Methuen).

Spradley, J. P., and Mann, B. J. (1975), *The Cocktail Waitress* (New York: Wiley).

Strauss, A. (1959), *Mirrors and Masks: The Search for Identity* (New York: The Free Press).

Sutherland, E. H. (1937), *The Professional Thief* (Chicago: Phoenix).

Van Gennep, A. (1960), *The Rites of Passage* (London: Routledge).

Which? (1968), Survey on people's attitudes to tipping, June (The Consumers Association).

Whyte, W. F. (ed.) (1946), *Industry and Society* (New York: McGraw-Hill).

Whyte, W.F. (1948), *Human Relations in the Restaurant Industry* (New York: Wiley).

Whyte, W. F. (1969), *Organizational Behaviour: Theory and Applications* (Homewood, Ill.: Irwin-Dorsey).

Whyte, W. F. (1970), *Street Corner Society* (6th ed. or later) (London: University of Chicago Press).

Woodbury, M. A. (1958), 'Ward dynamics and the formation of a therapeutic group', Chestnut Lodge Symposium. Rockville, Maryland, mimeo.

147

Index

148